THE UNITED NATIONS

Other Books in the At Issue Series:

1295
2/97

THE UNITED NATIONS

David Bender, *Publisher*
Bruno Leone, *Executive Editor*

Scott Barbour, *Managing Editor*
Brenda Stalcup, *Series Editor*

Karin L. Swisher, *Book Editor*

An Opposing Viewpoints ® Series

Greenhaven Press, Inc.
San Diego, California

Library of Congress Cataloging-in-Publication Data

The United Nations / Karin L. Swisher, book editor.
    p.   cm. — (At issue) (Opposing Viewpoints series)
    Includes bibliographical references and index.
    ISBN 1-56510-548-6 (lib. : alk. paper) — ISBN 1-56510-547-8
(pbk. : alk. paper)
    1. United Nations. 2. United Nations—United States.
I. Swisher, Karin L., 1966– . II. Series: Opposing Viewpoints
series (Unnumbered).
JX1977.U4255 1997
341.23—dc21   96-45364
                                                                        CIP

©1997 by Greenhaven Press, Inc., PO Box 289009,
San Diego, CA 92198-9009

Printed in the U.S.A.

Every effort has been made to trace owners of copyrighted material.

Table of Contents

Introduction

The United Nations was officially created when its charter was signed on June 26, 1945, by 51 countries, including the United States. The new international organization was the successor of the League of Nations, which had been formed by U.S. president Woodrow Wilson at the end of World War I in an attempt to prevent the kind of military aggression that might lead to future global conflicts. Unfortunately, the League had proved to be ineffective early on. Both Japan and Germany had withdrawn from the organization in the early 1930s and had later become the aggressors in World War II. Throughout 1943 and 1944, representatives from the United States, the Soviet Union, the United Kingdom, and China—allies during World War II—had met to discuss the formation of an international organization that would replace the League of Nations. At the end of the war, this organization—the United Nations—was formally established. The U.N. grew from 51 members in 1945 to 185 by its fiftieth anniversary in 1995.

The U.N.'s charter set out four primary goals: "to save succeeding generations from the scourge of war, which twice in our lifetime has brought untold sorrow to mankind . . . ; to reaffirm faith in fundamental human rights . . . ; to establish conditions under which justice and respect for the obligations arising from treaties and other sources of international law can be maintained; and to promote social progress and better standards of life in larger freedom." In order to promote these goals, the organizers established six different bodies. The Security Council, which consists of five permanent members (the United States, the United Kingdom, France, Russia, and China) and ten rotating member countries, was given primary responsibility for international peace and security. The General Assembly, to which all members belong, decides budgetary matters and votes on policy issues. The other bodies are the Secretariat, the Economic and Social Council, the Court of Justice, and the Trusteeship Council.

The United Nations' earliest priorities were nuclear arms control and disarmament, the protection of human rights, securing the independence of colonized countries, and the development of poorer countries. To control nuclear armaments, the U.N. promoted bans on nuclear testing, including undersea and space tests. It created the International Atomic Energy Agency in 1957 to promote the peaceful use of nuclear energy, and in 1968 it drafted the Non-Proliferation Treaty to halt the spread of nuclear weapons to more countries. The creation of the 1946 Commission on Human Rights led to the adoption of the Universal Declaration of Human Rights. In order to improve agriculture, health care, communications, and economic development, a number of specialized agencies were formed, including the U.N. Development Programme and the U.N. Conference on Trade and Development. The U.N. often functions in cooperation with other international organizations, such as the World Health Organization, the International Monetary Fund, and the World Trade Organization.

Though solving world health, population, development, and arms control problems is a large and vital part of the U.N. operation, many of the most current and strident debates have centered on peacekeeping, a term that appears nowhere in the U.N. charter but has always been the organization's foremost priority. The term "peacekeeping" was first used to describe the activities of the first U.N. observer mission in 1948, in which U.N. personnel were sent to the Middle East to prevent hostilities between the newly created state of Israel and its Arab neighbors. The first lightly armed peacekeeping mission was conducted in 1956 along the Suez Canal to create a buffer between Israel and Egypt. This mission lasted eleven years and involved nearly six thousand soldiers. Thirteen peacekeeping missions took place during the first forty-five years of the U.N.'s existence, the most successful of which was the 1960–1964 mission in the Belgian Congo, which assisted that nation's separation from colonial rule. Nearly twenty thousand troops were deployed to the Belgian Congo, coming close to the number sent on modern peacekeeping missions.

These missions adhered to the U.N. charter, which was originally designed to limit the level of involvement U.N. forces could undertake to secure peace. The U.N. is also limited by its pledge of noninterference in issues that are "essentially within the domestic jurisdiction of any states." As a result of this policy, certain guidelines have evolved concerning the deployment of U.N. peacekeeping forces. For example, a host government must consent to any U.N. deployment, as must the country contributing the troops to the mission. Any country with a particular interest in the outcome of a dispute is not allowed to participate in the peacekeeping mission. U.N. troops are allowed to use their weapons only in self-defense and must remain neutral if hostilities break out. If the criteria for U.N. involvement are not met, the U.N. cannot take direct action. Such was the case in the Korean War, which is now often considered a U.N. mission but was actually led and carried out by the United States and its allies. The Persian Gulf War was a similar action. Authorized by the U.N., a coalition made up of the United States, Great Britain, France, Saudi Arabia, and other countries repelled the Iraqi forces that had invaded Kuwait.

In the 1990s the United Nations has participated in missions in Haiti, Cyprus, the Western Sahara, Liberia, Somalia, India/Pakistan, Bosnia-Herzegovina, and the former Soviet republics of Georgia and Tajikistan, to name just a few. It is because of recent missions such as these, some of which the U.S. has participated in or led, that controversy has arisen over the scope of the U.N.'s responsibility for military-style peacekeeping. Many of these missions, particularly those in Bosnia and Somalia, have widely been considered ineffective or even outright failures.

Many of the earlier peacekeeping measures, critics and supporters alike note, were successful largely because the conflicts were usually interstate disputes between legitimate governments that welcomed U.N. involvement. According to Raymond Carroll, a former editor at *Newsweek* and author of *The Future of the UN*, in most cases

> both sides wanted the UN forces to be there, wanted the shooting to halt and were in command of disciplined military forces. The parties to the conflict were recognized countries, members of the UN, who respected the missions of the men in the blue helmets, soldiers who used their weapons only in self-defense.

Few of the more recent conflicts share these characteristics, however. Current conflicts are more likely to involve two or more parties within a single state, rather than separate nations at war. Carroll maintains that these conflicts "are likely to be partly ethnic, religious or secessionist in nature, or they may be factional disputes among purely domestic rivals." The more recent peace-keeping efforts have often failed because, in many of the troubled regions, governments have broken down, combatants have been unwilling to cease fighting, and U.N. troops have been unwelcome. Essentially, the organization and structure of U.N. peacekeeping has remained static while the nature of world conflict has changed.

Many of those who criticize the U.N.'s more recent peacekeeping efforts point to the disastrous shelling of U.N. troops in Bosnia by the Serbs in the early 1990s. Critics insist that the attack, in which U.N. troops were unable to fight back effectively, is proof that the U.N. is ill equipped for military missions. Some contend that the organization is not only ill equipped but that it was never intended to function as a military entity or to enter ongoing conflict situations for either humanitarian or peacekeeping reasons. *Disarmament Times* editor and U.N. journalist Jim Wurst asserts that the U.N. "has dangerously blurred the line between peacekeeping (working to stabilize a truce) and peace enforcement (the current jargon for fighting), as well as the line between military and humanitarian actions."

Criticism of U.S. involvement in U.N. peacekeeping operations has also become more intense, in part as a result of recent failures. The 1992 invasion of Somalia by the United States, under the auspices of the U.N., is often cited by critics as an example of why the United States should avoid involvement in U.N. missions. The United States initially invaded Somalia to provide humanitarian aid to relieve a severe countrywide famine, which had been caused in part by the disruption of food distribution by several competing factions. The famine was successfully halted, and the United Nations took full command in 1993. The U.N., along with American forces, stayed to try to rebuild Somalia's infrastructure (hospitals, civil services, police force, and educational system), but local leaders, and their heavily armed followers, objected violently to the U.N.'s continued presence. Several soldiers were killed, including a number of Americans. The body of one American was shown on the evening news being dragged through the streets of Somalia's capital. Ultimately both the United States and the United Nations left Somalia, leaving it largely in chaos. After this experience, many American politicians and foreign policy experts were more convinced than ever that the United States should refrain from sending American troops on U.N. missions. California representative Andrea Seastrand sums up the views of many critics of America's involvement in U.N. operations: "This entangling alliance with the world body and its web of specialized agencies and institutions has resulted in our involvement in one foreign quarrel after another, from Korea to Vietnam to Bosnia. We have paid dearly, in terms of blood, treasure and potential loss of sovereignty."

While Somalia is universally acknowledged as a military failure, supporters of the United Nations assert that the primary goal of that mission—to end the famine—was accomplished. Supporters also contend that it is shortsighted to argue that a few difficult or failed missions prove that the greater goal of keeping the peace is no longer worthwhile. They maintain that intrastate conflicts that produce floods of refugees, famine, and genocide violate the "moral conscience" of the world, if not specifically the U.N.'s charter. These supporters of U.N. intervention suggest, for example, that the genocide in Rwanda in 1994 could have been halted or even prevented had the now gun-shy United Nations intervened sooner. More than five hundred thousand people were killed in Rwanda during a struggle for power between members of two rival ethnic factions. Hundreds of thousands more poured across the borders into neighboring countries, straining their economies and threatening to drag them into the fight, which ultimately could have destabilized the entire region. U.N. supporters contend that fear of another Bosnia- or Somalia-style failure hampered a timely U.N. intervention in that conflict.

Lincoln P. Bloomfield, a professor emeritus of political science at the Massachusetts Institute of Technology, asserts that many of the United Nations' members have collectively concluded that enforced famine, terror, racial genocide, and other atrocities are unacceptable, violating the spirit of the U.N. charter. Bloomfield and others argue that these situations necessitate an international response similar to those of earlier, more circumscribed missions. The U.N. response to these new kinds of international crises should, according to Bloomfield,

> feature compliance procedures that resemble a process of *law enforcement*. It will look less like a traditional binary choice between war or peace and more like a step process that mimics domestic *policing*. Violations of agreed rules will take many forms along a broad continuum, matched by a continuum of community responses.

Many of those who support continued U.N. involvement in peacekeeping efforts around the world also clearly support continued American involvement in those efforts. The United States is generally considered to be the only remaining superpower, whose leadership in conflict situations is necessary. Within the United States, supporters argue that U.S. involvement in the United Nations allows America to promote its own economic and political interests abroad without appearing to be heavy-handed or the "world's policeman." The U.S. ambassador to the United Nations, Madeleine K. Albright, supports this view and contends that joint peacekeeping efforts cost the United States less and involve fewer American troops than do unilateral efforts. The Center for Defense Information, a defense analysis organization in Washington, D.C., asserts:

> The U.S. can, at significantly less cost, wield great influence over world events and achieve U.S. policy goals by remaining fully engaged in planning and implementing UN peace operations. Not only is such engagement cheaper, it allows us the luxury of influencing events with minimal commitment of U.S. military personnel.

The center concludes that the United States must continue to be involved in U.N. peacekeeping.

The debates over U.N. peacekeeping operations will likely continue as new conflicts arise and old ones simmer. This is only one of several controversies in which the U.N. remains embroiled. International calls for fiscal and organizational reform are as loud as the criticisms of peacekeeping, with some accusing the U.N. of incompetence or even outright corruption. In addition, the United Nations has become a central target of many right-wing militias and others who assert that the international body threatens the freedom and sovereignty of the United States. These and other issues are discussed and debated in *At Issue: The United Nations*. This anthology reveals that after more than fifty years, opinion regarding the U.N.'s structure and mission is far from unanimous.

1

The United Nations Must Be Radically Reformed

Stefan Halper

Stefan Halper, a former White House and State Department official, is a nationally syndicated columnist and an analyst for the Cato Institute, a libertarian think tank in Washington, D.C.

The United Nations currently receives billions of dollars each year from its member states and conducts development, aid, and peace-keeping projects all over the world without stringent oversight of either its projects or its accounts. Consequently, abuses range from incompetence to corruption to outright theft. If it is to remain in existence, the United Nations must be reformed to ensure that it is held financially and politically accountable for its actions.

The United Nations is under increasing attack by critics in the United States and other countries. At the heart of the organization's mounting problems is an almost total lack of accountability, which gives rise to suspicions of wholesale corruption. Existing evidence indicates that corruption and mismanagement go beyond the routine fraud, waste, and abuse of resources that mark all public-sector enterprises.

UN budgets are shrouded in secrecy, and the actual performance of the myriad bureaucracies is translucent, if not opaque. There is no reliable way to determine whether the various and often competing specialized agencies (at least two dozen UN agencies are involved in food and agricultural policy) are doing their jobs, and many UN activities, even if they are of some value, can be carried out better and more efficiently by other groups. Other activities should not be undertaken at all.

Available evidence coupled with the United Nations' unwillingness to undergo a thorough audit raise serious questions about its mission and the means used to carry it out. Secretary General Boutros Boutros-Ghali's rationale that the world body is accountable to all its 185 member-states is meaningless. Such an amorphous standard of accountability is akin to saying no one is responsible.

The United Nations is in dire need of reform, starting with a compre-

Stefan Halper, "A Miasma of Corruption: The United Nations Turns Fifty," *Cato Policy Analysis*, April 30, 1996. Reprinted by permission of the Cato Institute.

hensive, independent audit. Even if a complete audit were performed, however, there is no guarantee anything would be done about the problems identified. And radical change may not be possible, no matter how obvious the need. Given all the earlier, failed attempts to put things right, even on a limited basis, optimism about meaningful reform may be an exercise in wishful thinking.

The United Nations' 50th birthday came and went in 1995, and while some people treated the event as a celebration, others were far less enthusiastic. Indeed, there was decidedly more derision than congratulation in the United States. That would have seemed odd only a few years ago. Few in the attentive public then thought the United Nations was in need of serious, much less radical, reform. To the contrary, with the end of the Cold War, most Americans, especially members of the opinion-shaping elites, regarded the United Nations as more relevant than ever. By the organization's golden anniversary, however, criticism was being expressed even by UN sympathizers in the Clinton administration, who view themselves as modern internationalists parrying the thrusts of uncouth Philistine isolationists. Suddenly, it seemed, critics of the United Nations were no longer confined to the flat-earth faction of the political right, which had long considered the body a world government in the making. The recent relatively mild critiques from the foreign policy establishment, though, are woefully overdue and understated.

Frustration with the UN

An increasing center of frustration with UN failures can be found in the U.S. Congress. Some members have even called for U.S. withdrawal from the world body and the expulsion of the organization from its New York City headquarters. And the arguments of the abolitionists are getting a respectful hearing from the mainstream press.[1]

An American withdrawal would almost certainly mean the collapse of the United Nations. Without the generous, if unwilling, support of U.S. taxpayers, the United Nations would face imminent financial ruin. A decision to leave the world body may still be a decade or so away, but disgust with the United Nations is growing, not receding. Recent and expensive peacekeeping failures in Angola, Cambodia, Bosnia, and Somalia have greatly fueled the discontent.[2]

The Clinton administration's early, naive hope that the United States could offload nettlesome foreign conflicts on the United Nations—by sending American troops, who would serve under international command, to second that body's efforts—seems far more remote than 1993, when it was first suggested. But the rapid fading of the administration's early dreams is a measure of the current pessimism about the United Nations and its multitude of agencies that, with little rhyme or reason, have over the decades grown like "a coral reef," in the words of John Bolton, former assistant secretary of state for international organizations.[3]

In June 1995 on the stage of San Francisco's War Memorial Opera House, distinguished speakers from around the world, including President Clinton, labored mightily to echo the hopes expressed for the United Nations by its founders in June 1945 at the organization's charter-signing ceremony, attended by President Harry Truman. The anniversary efforts, however, fell flat. The contrast in rhetoric between the American presidents was instructive. Truman spoke glowingly of ending war through collective security, a hope anchored to the expectation of continuing the wartime alliance in perpetuity. In contrast, Clinton spoke defensively of reforming the middle-aged organization to fend off the "new isolationists" supposedly hungering for the kill. He did not even mention Bosnia, the United Nations' most recent and visible collective security mission.[4]

UN budgets are shrouded in secrecy, and the actual performance of the myriad bureaucracies is translucent, if not opaque.

Reforming the United Nations, coupled with a less exalted vision of what it might usefully do in the next century, is now safely within the mainstream of American "informed" discussion of the world body. The prevailing assumption underlying much of the talk is that the organization is in trouble, but its problems are fixable: budgets and bureaucracies can be trimmed; waste, duplication, and fraud can be uncovered and eliminated; and finances can be put on a sounder basis. Moderate reformers also concede that peacekeeping missions need to be more carefully defined and that there should be less talk and more action, particularly in connection with humanitarian services. And what if such steps are not taken? Unfortunately, that question is rarely addressed.

Any prescriptions for measured reform may well be much too little and much, much too late. After all, as members of Congress on both sides of the aisle well know, previous attempts at correcting the United Nations' many failings have come largely to naught. The most significant congressional effort at overhaul was the so-called Kassebaum-Solomon amendment passed in 1985. That measure required the United States to reduce its 25 percent share of the general UN budget to 20 percent unless a weighted system of voting on budget matters was introduced in the General Assembly. The legislation did spark some attempts at cutting spending and reducing the number of top administrators, but in general the United Nations has ignored or evaded the clear purpose of Kassebaum-Solomon.[5]

Such a frustrating record suggests that the problems may be inherent and irredeemable rather than incidental and correctable. It also implies that the United Nations as constituted is so fundamentally corrupt that no redesign, no matter how clever the blueprint, would ever be carried out. Although that suspicion is not yet in the mainstream of debate, it deserves a careful hearing. But first we need to understand how the United Nations has gotten itself in the perhaps irreparable fix it is in.

The UN family and how it grew

American Wilsonian internationalists saw the United Nations as a second—and perhaps final—chance to create a world body that would preserve the peace through collective security. President Wilson's plea for U.S. membership in the League of Nations—which he could have gotten with a few minor compromises with the Senate—was rebuffed by that body. Wilson's ideological heirs believed that the lack of U.S. participation was the league's fatal flaw, leading to its ineffectiveness in dealing with the wave of aggression in the 1930s.

There is actually little evidence to support that contention.[6] Nevertheless, the Wilsonian analysis persuaded a generation of American policymakers and opinion makers that the lack of an effective world organization was the root cause of World War II. Moreover, with the arrival of the atomic age, creation of a capable global security organization seemed, not an exercise in idealism, but a stark need. Either a UN-based system of collective security would be forged by the wartime allies—large and small alike—or the planet's history would come to a swift and ugly end. To make sure that the latter would not happen, the UN Security Council—in effect, its five permanent members—was given the power to decide what measures should be taken in case of a threat to the peace. In contrast, the league's council could make recommendations for action that individual member states were free to ignore.[7]

Available evidence coupled with the United Nations' unwillingness to undergo a thorough audit raise serious questions about its mission and the means used to carry it out.

Hopes for an effective United Nations became an early casualty of the Cold War. Any peace-preserving action could be stalled in the Security Council by a Soviet veto, while General Assembly resolutions passed under the aegis of the United States could be simply ignored by Moscow and its growing list of satellites.[8]

Nevertheless, the United States doggedly sought to use the organization whenever possible. Truman, for example, insisted on a UN role as a collective guarantor of the Korean peninsula's security. That was obtained, but only after a major diplomatic effort to persuade reluctant allies to join in the effort to repel North Korea's armed aggression in June 1950. (A fortuitous Soviet boycott of the Security Council prevented a veto of the UN "police action.") Later, when Stalin sent back his representative, the United States obtained what it needed to continue the mission through a constitutionally dubious Uniting for Peace resolution passed by the then-friendly General Assembly. Under that resolution, the General Assembly would assume the powers of the Security Council when the latter body was stymied by the veto of a permanent member.

The transformation of UN membership

All of that, of course, was possible only because the United States enjoyed the support of a majority in the 51-member General Assembly. That margin vanished forever in the mid-1950s when a momentary thaw in U.S.-Soviet relations following the death of Stalin allowed the admission of 20 new members. Five years later the General Assembly had 82 members, nearly all former colonies of the European powers.[9] By 1970 the number had jumped yet again to 108; by 1980 it was 136; and by 1995 the General Assembly had a total of 185 member-states, each with one vote.

The vastly expanded General Assembly was soon dominated by non-Western states whose elites seldom shared the political culture of the democratic West, much less any belief in market economics. The new majority felt free to exercise its power by passing resolutions favorable to the Third World and its member-states' various pet projects. Although the Third World was hardly homogeneous, operating on an identical agenda, a mutually convenient system of logrolling soon came into being. For example, Arab states would vote for black African resolutions against South African apartheid, provided that the black African countries in turn voted against Israel when called upon to do so. All factions frequently voted against the United States, although they were seldom as harsh with the Soviet Union—as President John F. Kennedy discovered when the non-aligned states refused to condemn the USSR for resuming aboveground nuclear tests in September 1961.[10]

Placing financial burdens on the United States

Nowhere was the power of the new majority in the General Assembly more evident than in the critical area of finance. In 1945 the United States was assessed 39.98 percent of the UN budget, while the poorest members were each assessed a minimum of 0.04 percent. Although the U.S. assessment eventually dropped to 25 percent for the general budget, that decline is not as large as the decline in America's share of global economic output. The U.S. share of the peacekeeping budget, which is usually larger than the general budget, remains 31 percent. The UN budget is actually three budgets: regular, peacekeeping, and voluntary contributions (which cover humanitarian and development programs). The total cost comes to some $10.5 billion a year.[11] Moreover, the General Assembly's financial bias in favor of Third World members has become more pronounced over the decades. The General Assembly reduced the assessment for poor states to 0.02 percent in 1973 and then cut it again to a minuscule 0.01 percent five years later.[12]

By 1992, 79 members were paying the minimum amount to the regular budget while another 9 were chipping in 0.02 percent. That meant that a majority of voting members in the General Assembly contributed less than 1 percent of the UN's general budget while just 14 members contributed 84 percent. A similar situation prevails with the peacekeeping budget.[13] That fundamental disconnect between power and the purse is the central factor in the corruption of the United Nations and has led to a proliferation of agencies, an oversized bureaucracy, and general irresponsibility.

From swords into plowshares into jobs for the boys

There is no need for romanticism about the Third World. Those who saw those nations as poor and exploited—and therefore virtuous—were hopelessly out of touch with reality. Third World countries may be poor, but the elites that run them are decidedly not. Nor does their rule very often rest on the consent of the governed, even in theory. Although democratic rule has spread a bit in the post–Cold War era, the most dramatic gains for democracy have been in the former communist Second World and Latin America, which never quite fit into the *tiers monde* where Asian warlords feel comfortable rubbing shoulders with Middle Eastern and African military dictators at meetings of the Non-Aligned Movement and the UN General Assembly.

The opaque budgetary process

A kleptocratic culture of nonaccountability at home was easily transferred to the world body. How it was managed is less clearly understood. That is because UN budgetary procedures have for decades been covered by a shroud of obfuscation and secrecy—all unnecessary for an international organization that is supported in great part by American and Western taxpayers.

Two observers well versed in the ways of the United Nations summarize its budgetary process as follows:

> A draft two-year program budget is proposed by the Secretary-General to the General Assembly. Prior to the Assembly's discussions, this draft budget is reviewed by the intergovernmental Committee for Program and Coordination and the 16-member expert Advisory Committee on Administrative and Budgetary Questions. Apprised of the comments and recommendations of these two bodies, the General Assembly and its Fifth (Administrative and Budgetary) Committee carry out an in-depth scrutiny of the budget, which goes through two readings in the Fifth Committee and one final reading in the plenary of the Assembly. A few years ago, formal agreement was reached by the General Assembly that the budget must be passed by consensus and cannot be adopted by a vote.[14]

The requirement for consensus supposedly cured the problem of the many poor members' arriving at a budget paid for by the few rich.

In reality, the above description of the budgetary process is more anatomical than physiological. By the time the budget is formally considered by the General Assembly, nearly all the decisions have been made within bodies dominated by the Third World majority. The Committee for Program and Coordination is a prime example of the problem. As a result of U.S. congressional pressure for reform of the UN's finances, that committee was established with 21 members in December 1986. It was supposed to give major donors a larger say on the budget. But within two years the membership expanded to 34, thereby once again giving the Third World states a dominant voice on budgetary questions. Moreover, there is scant evidence that the major contributors seek to exert much influence on the committee.

An equally serious problem is the opaqueness of the budget process itself.[15] Nowhere is that more evident than in the workings of the Advisory·Committee on Administrative and Budgetary Questions, which for more than 20 years has been run by Conrad S.M. Mselle of Tanzania. According to *New York Times* correspondent Christopher Wren,

> No outsider can explain how decisions get made because Mr. Mselle, who has no formal training in finance, convenes committee meetings behind closed doors. "This is not nuclear science, this is financial stuff," a diplomat said. "There's no reason for it to operate in secrecy."[16]

Of course, there is a reason for that secrecy; it just does not happen to be a legitimate one. The secrecy allows Mselle to do pretty much what he wants with other people's money. That includes rewarding himself with a tax-free income of $134,000 a year as well as a $60,000 salary paid to what the *New York Times* euphemistically refers to as Mselle's "companion." The lack of transparency and accountability of the Advisory Committee's decisions, policies, and procedures is replicated throughout the United Nations.[17]

Bureaucracy run amok

Since the Third World majority took control of the United Nations and its budget, total UN employment has ballooned from 1,500 to more than 50,000 worldwide. The latter figure does not include the nearly 10,000 consultants or the peacekeeping forces, which at their height in 1993 numbered some 80,000. No exact figure on total employment including consultants—the hiring of consultants is a popular and much-abused practice at the United Nations—can be given. That is because until 1994 there was no central, computerized list of personnel. Even today there are no records of many appointments in the Secretariat.[18]

The personnel costs (including generous pension benefits) of that army of bureaucrats consume an estimated 70 percent or more of the UN operating budget. Given the lack of transparency, the percentage could be even higher. That leaves relatively few financial resources for the actual missions of the United Nations and its specialized agencies, including the organization's much-touted humanitarian programs.

The salary and benefits packages of UN employees based in New York City are incredibly lucrative. Statistics compiled in 1995 revealed that the average annual salary for a midlevel accountant at the United Nations was $84,500. The salary for a comparable position in non-UN businesses and agencies was $41,964. A UN computer analyst could expect to receive $111,500 compared to $56,836 paid counterparts outside the UN bureaucracy. An assistant secretary general received $190,250; the mayor of New York City was paid $130,000.[19] The raw figures do not convey the extent of the disparity, however, since the salaries of UN employees are *free of all taxes*. In addition to their bloated salaries, UN bureaucrats enjoy an array of costly perks, including monthly rent subsidies of up to $3,800 and annual education grants (also tax-free) of $12,675 per child. The UN pension program is so generous that entry-level staffers whose pay rises only as fast as inflation can retire in 30 years with $1.8 million.[20]

The United Nations is in dire need of reform, starting with a comprehensive, independent audit.

But it is not numbers alone that should be of concern. There is the question of quality of personnel. Unlike the old League of Nations, the United Nations has never developed a well-trained international civil service. By nearly all accounts, a very few men and women struggle to do most of the real work. The rest are time servers whose sloth is reputed to be of mythic proportions. Secretary General Boutros-Ghali, shortly after assuming his post, remarked that until he acquired his present position he had thought the Egyptian bureaucracy was the most inefficient in the world. He was, he admitted, quite wrong. The secretary general also has estimated that perhaps half of the UN workforce does nothing useful.[21] Even when work is done, it is often unnecessary. For example, according to Richard Thornburgh, who once served as under secretary general, "In the Office of Conference Services where translation services are provided, we currently employ 500 secretary-stenographers who are given the responsibility of typing the dictated version of translated documents and returning them to the translators for editing and approval." Those positions, of course, could be eliminated entirely if the translators worked with word processors. The cost of that featherbedding is $20 million a year.[22]

There is no mystery about the pervasive lack of efficiency. The bulk of UN employees worldwide are drawn from the Third World and the now-defunct Soviet bloc, although bureaucrats from the West certainly are not immune to the temptations of sloth. Many have no particular skills other than cultivating support from their sponsoring governments. Once they are inside the UN bureaucracy, it is virtually impossible to fire them. At best, a conscientious manager (there are a few) can force the lateral transfer of an especially unsatisfactory subordinate. Most managers, however, do not bother even making the attempt.

Given the current rules, it is nearly impossible to correct such problems. One reason is that, in blatant disregard of sound management principles, the United Nations has no functioning system of personnel evaluation. Although employees are supposedly rated on their job performance, nearly everyone receives an excellent rating—some 90 percent, in fact, during a recent year—which makes evaluations virtually meaningless. All attempts to change that nonsystem of evaluation have failed—despite five separate efforts since the 1970s—and for good reason. Few within the United Nations want the appalling practice ended. Ending it would challenge the decades-old policy of corrupt hiring practices, which a majority of member-states have no interest in correcting since they directly benefit from the status quo.[23] An irresponsible, unaccountable bureaucracy that does not even meet minimal requirements for any professional civil service is the wellspring of many of the other evils that make the United Nations such a corrupt institution.

Waste, fraud, and abuse

That brings us to the question of corruption narrowly defined, that is, the well-known unholy trinity of waste, fraud, and abuse. There is abundant anecdotal evidence of all three being committed within the UN system. For example, the UN Children's Fund lost perhaps $10 million thanks to mismanagement in Kenya. Nearly $4 million in cash was stolen outright at UN headquarters in Mogadishu, Somalia. And lest anyone think that such examples are confined to UN operations in Africa, consider this recent report from the *New York Times*:

> Nearly $497,000 earmarked for a two-week conference on the Sustainable Development of Small Island Developing States in Barbados last year included $15,000 to fly in representatives of a "national liberation movement" recognized by the Organization of African Unity. In fact,

the movement was Polisario from Western Sahara, a desert region conspicuously short of small islands.[24]

Examples from the corrupt culture of the United Nations could be multiplied almost endlessly, but that dreary record would still avoid the central questions: just how much waste, fraud, and abuse is there in the United Nations; and is it really no worse than in other public bureaucracies, as UN apologists often contend? As to the latter question, bureaucracies vary considerably in their honesty and effectiveness. Anyone comparing the efficiency and rectitude of Chad's public sector to Wisconsin's state government would come up with striking results. In any case, the United Nations, which purports to be the conscience of the international community, should be held to the highest ethical standards. It should at least be judged on the same basis as the bureaucracy of its predecessor, the League of Nations. On that basis, the comparison is extremely unfavorable.[25]

The quest for an inspector general

The larger question of exactly how much corruption exists cannot be answered with precision for the simple reason that the United Nations has never been subjected or subjected itself to a thorough, top-to-bottom audit. The UN Secretariat's Internal Audit Division has long been a toothless lion. Its small staff has no jurisdiction over the autonomous agencies, and its powers over the Secretariat itself are minimal. The auditors rely totally on information supplied by managers; the guilty are never identified by name; and the results are kept confidential. It is no wonder that the Internal Audit Division usually discovers only the most petty fraud.[26]

Until 1995, in fact, the United Nations lacked an inspector general's office, despite repeated urgings of supporters and critics alike. Moreover, the under secretary general for administration and management had been replaced seven times in eight years until Joseph Connor, a former Price Waterhouse executive, took over in mid-1994. Until Connor's appointment, the job had been held mostly by political appointees, many of whom were inherently disinterested in management. One of those officials spent most of his time in Namibia arranging its independence from South African control.[27]

A decision [by America] to leave the world body may still be a decade or so away, but disgust with the United Nations is growing, not receding.

The rather obvious and much-needed appointment of a management specialist to the post came only after a steady drumbeat of criticism, in particular the March 1993 report of the then under secretary general for administration and management, former U.S. attorney general Richard Thornburgh. Thornburgh issued a report that advocated the establishment of an inspector general with real powers, because the existing auditing system under the General Assembly's Joint Inspection Unit was found to be "totally lacking" in effectiveness. It was understaffed as well as a patronage "dumping ground" bent on such dubious projects as a $4 million study on "Managing Works of Art in the United Nations." In other words, the Thornburgh report concluded that the Joint Inspection Unit was no better than the offices and agencies on which it was supposed to keep tabs.[28]

In its place, Thornburgh recommended creating a "strong" inspector general's office, "a common set of accounting principles and standards," a code of conduct that would "compel full financial disclosure by senior management" to prevent conflicts of interest, and an "overhaul of the performance evaluation process."[29] Incredibly, all of those elementary principles of sound management had been absent since the beginning of the United Nations.

Most of the sensible reforms proposed in the Thornburgh report have been ignored. One that could not be easily dodged, however, was appointment of an inspector general, an idea that quickly attracted interest in the increasingly frustrated U.S. Congress. Consequently, in 1995 a new unit under the secretary general, Internal Oversight Services, presided over by yet another under secretary general—German diplomat Karl Theodore Paschke—was established.[30]

Tepid reform: the appointment of an inspector general

The impetus for the decision to finally create an inspector general's office and appoint a director not controlled by the dominant Third World faction did not, of course, originate with the United Nations itself. Instead, in April 1994, an impatient Capitol Hill demanded the reform "or else." The "else" was a threat to withhold $420 million of the U.S. assessment from the financially strapped organization until the demand was fully complied with. The congressional requirement called for an independent inspector general with wide-ranging powers whose reports could not be censored by the secretary general. Moreover, whistle blowers were to be provided ample protection—correcting another long-standing weak point in the alleged system of UN accountability.

Unfortunately, but not surprisingly, the General Assembly recrafted the congressional requirements and diluted the potential effectiveness of the new post. The General Assembly was able to weaken the reform effort thanks in large part to the refusal of Clinton administration negotiators to stay the course. What the General Assembly finally created was an inspector general with less than autonomous and sweeping powers. For example, the inspector general's budget would not be independent and he would serve at the pleasure of the secretary general—an unmistakable sign of dependence. Nor was Paschke given the power to correct any wrongdoing that he found, much less threaten offenders with criminal proceedings.[31]

Lifting the rock—barely: the inspector general's first report

Such dilution of authority has contributed to the highly limited nature of the inspector general's first report, completed seven months after his appointment in March 1995. Short on time, funds, and staff, that initial attempt at cost accounting at the United Nations—a first after 50 years— produced little surprise, much less shock. Yet even that limited effort is reported to have "demoralized" much of the organization's staff.[32] Paschke made no pretense that he could clean the Augean stable in seven months—a Herculean task that would require years in any case. Therefore, he concentrated on several priorities: peacekeeping, humanitarian services, and procurement. A further narrowing of focus limited his investigation to abuse that constituted outright theft. That limitation, of course, left out such concerns as duplication and inappropriateness of efforts and overall accountability. But even that first, limited swipe uncovered $16.8 million in outright fraud and waste. The following were chief among his findings, according to one *New York Times* report.

- In Somalia, $369,000 was paid for fuel distribution services that a contractor did not provide.
- A project director for the United Nations Relief and Works Agency, which helps Palestinian refugees, kept $100,000 of agency money in his private bank account and failed to disclose a personal stake in the irrigation project under way.
- In Nairobi, a staff member of the United Nations Center for Human Settlements arranged loans worth $98,000 for a company in which she had been a partner, and with whose director she was "closely associated."
- A travel assistant working in New York for the special commission that supervises the dismantling of Iraq's nuclear weapons program misappropriated $28,000 in travelers checks.[33]

The report also contained the usual criticisms of poor management practices and abysmal personnel policy. But Paschke's overall conclusion proved more disturbing to the cause of real reform than any of his criticisms. The inspector general stated, "I have not found the UN to be a more corrupt organization, an organization that shows more fraud than any other comparable public organization."[34]

Any prescriptions for measured reform may well be much too little and much, much too late.

But what is a comparable organization? Certainly not the old League of Nations, whose standards were very high. The statement, in short, has a ring of self-serving complacency, precisely what the United Nations does not need if it is to survive. Members of Congress had hoped for an inspector general who would prove to be a "junkyard dog," but U.S. ambassador to the United Nations Madeleine Albright—no UN buster— suggested that Paschke had thus far proved to be a "junkyard puppy."[35]

The Internal Oversight Services Office, in short, may well become another typical UN effort to deflect criticism without addressing the central problem. In any event, there is likely to be ongoing controversy and further attempts, at least on Capitol Hill, to make the United Nations responsible and responsive to its major contributors.

Can the United Nations be reformed?

There is no end to the schemes proposed for reforming the United Nations; many of them bubbled up in and around the institution's 50th anniversary. Unfortunately, most approach the issue from the wrong assumption: that the chief problem is a lack of money. To be sure, many nations "owe" billions—the United States, in particular, which is now $1.2 billion in arrears. That is hardly a new situation. In September 1993, for example, some 116 countries were behind in their payments while only 62 were paid in full. Two years later little had changed. At the end of December 1995, 91 of 185 members had not paid their share of the regular UN budget.[36] In 1993 a blue-ribbon panel sponsored by the Ford Foundation and presided over by Paul Volcker, former chairman of the U.S. Federal Reserve, and Shijuro Ogata, former deputy governor of the Bank of Japan, proposed to resolve the United Nations' cash-flow problems through a variety of means. The panel's principal recommendation was that past dues and present ones be paid in four quarterly installments, "instead of a single lump sum in the beginning of the year."[37]

The independent revenue panacea

More recently, the secretary general has suggested that the cure for the United Nations' financial woes is to give the world body taxing power. That would enable the organization to raise revenues directly and would give the institution an unprecedented degree of independence. Indeed, it would greatly diminish, if not eliminate, the financial control possessed (at least theoretically) by the member-states. Suggestions such as imposing a surcharge on international airline tickets or charging a fee for foreign exchange transactions—which amount to between $1 trillion and $1.5 trillion per day—have been met with scant interest in the Clinton administration and open hostility in the Republican-controlled Congress.[38]

Critics have raised the red flag of world government in response to proposals for taxing authority. But a more realistic objection is that such schemes would enhance the corrupt nature of the United Nations, whose core defect is an utter lack of accountability. The United Nations certainly is not accountable to its most important financial contributor, the United States, nor to the other major powers that largely provide the remaining share of the money. Nor can accountability be found with the secretary general, the chief administrative officer according to the UN Charter. Occupants of that post have regularly pleaded that they cannot be held accountable—none more emphatically than the incumbent, who contends that the member-nations are all-powerful in questions of responsibility.[39] Freeing the United Nations of any form of control by the major contributors would make that problem worse, not better.

The General Assembly's financial bias in favor of Third World members has become more pronounced over the decades.

Since the negative reaction to the secretary general's proposals for raising new revenues, he has tried another tack. This time he has proposed to reduce the U.S. share of the general budget from the current 25 percent to 15 or 20 percent. In addition, he has in hand a recommendation from his management experts to cut the UN Secretariat staff based in New York by 1,150 positions.[40] Such suggestions come at a very late date and merely reflect the growing pressure on the United Nations from the U.S. Congress, among others. Moreover, the steps are modest ones—the UN specialized agencies, for example, would not shrink at all—and do not address the larger question of accountability. Why U.S. officials should be satisfied with such half measures, even if they were to be implemented, is very much an open question.

A radical reform agenda

How can the United Nations be made accountable in a meaningful sense of the term? Before addressing that primary question, however, we need to spell out the realistic options facing the organization. There are only two. The United Nations must either be radically reformed and its various bodies and agencies made strictly accountable to their primary donors, or failing that—and the record of failed reform attempts warrants pessimism—the principal donors, especially the United States, should end any further obligation to support financially an organization that is inherently corrupt and unfixable. The Reagan administration's withdrawal from the United Nations Educational, Scientific, and Cultural Organization in 1984 is a model of what could be done.

There must be an agreement among the major donors that a thorough housecleaning is in order. The United States could theoretically pursue that project alone, but without the cooperation of the Japanese, Russians, Germans, French, British, and to a much lesser extent, the Chinese, the UN bureaucracy, as in the past, would be well positioned to stymie a grand audit.

That audit must be carried out by a properly staffed, completely independent inspector general with a warrant allowing complete access to all UN and related-agency records. Indeed, some of the worst waste and duplication can be found in the affiliated agencies. For example, at least two dozen UN agencies are involved in food and agricultural policy, including one of the most notoriously ill managed, the Food and Agricultural Organization.[41] The proliferation of bureaucratic entities and the lack of pruning of obsolete ones is evident throughout the United Nations; agencies, councils, committees, and other bureaucratic bric-a-brac once established are almost never eliminated even though their usefulness has long since come to an end. The Trusteeship Council, for example, still absorbs resources even though it no longer has any wards.[42]

The lack of organizational coherence that characterizes the United Nations generally is especially striking in the affiliated agencies—which spend the largest share of the overall UN budget. Consider this observation by one seasoned diplomatic correspondent:

> The chiefs of some autonomous UN agencies rule their fiefdoms like autocrats, answering to no one. Regional mafias of UN bureaucrats have taken root, consolidating their power through favoritism in hiring and promotions. Recipient governments also routinely plunder UN programs, diverting aid from intended beneficiaries with little remonstration from UN agencies.[43]

A comprehensive audit cannot be completed in haste and could well take up to five years to finish. Moreover, the scope of the inquiry cannot be limited to fraud, waste, and outright theft, narrowly defined. Rather, the approach should be that of zero-based budgeting, both financially and conceptually. In other words, the audit needs to determine, not only whether the various bodies are effectively performing their missions, but also whether a particular mission is worth pursuing in the first place.

Curbing pretentious conferences

One of the most egregious abuses is the United Nations' penchant for holding international conferences of dubious worth. A splendid example was 1995's $2.5 million Summit for Social Development held in Copenhagen, Denmark. Featuring 100 world leaders, the summit (and its dozen preparatory meetings) fuzzily focused on poverty, job creation, and "solidarity." The outcome was roughly divisible into two categories: bromides that few could quarrel with or find of practical use and proposals for yet more government intervention to promote societal betterment.[44]

The UN conference that fretted about "social issues" was matched by huge conferences on women in Beijing in 1995, population control in Cairo in 1994, and, of course, the Rio environmental summit in 1992. All attracted thousands of delegates who were usually pursuing agendas associated with the statist left. Although few results can be pointed to—resolutions passed are not binding, fortunately, on anyone—there is little indication, considering the sponsors and the size of the attendance, that any serious work can ever be achieved at such gatherings. As a result, even boosters of the United Nations (including the Clinton administration) are growing critical of the proliferation of high-profile conferences. Said one unnamed senior U.S. official, "We think the General Assembly, which includes all 185 UN member states, is the proper forum for addressing these issues, and it's time to stop running around the world wasting resources when the same work could be done right here in New York at much less cost."[45]

Alternative organizations

A reform audit should also examine whether some of the functions of the United Nations can be carried out more efficiently by other organizations. We are no longer living in the world of 1945. In the last 50 years private, volunteer organizations and state-run agencies (the U.S. Peace Corps, the British Volunteer Service) have sprung up like mushrooms. Many are vastly more efficient than (often) rival UN agencies, which are top-heavy with bad management and provide relatively few dollars for actual humanitarian relief even when those funds are not diverted to other less worthy causes by host governments. It is not heartless to no longer accept at face value what bureaucrats claim they do for the world's poor and suffering. A vivid example of the collective wisdom about the UN humanitarian mission was the General Assembly's approval in 1984 of a $73.5 million regional conference center in Addis Ababa, Ethiopia. That decision was made at a time when the murderous regime of Mengistu Haile-Mariam had induced a massive famine that left international relief agencies scrambling for donations.[46] Scarce resources wasted, and therefore not available to help those in need, serve no legitimate purpose.

A thorough scrutiny of the largely unexamined and unaudited UN budgets would allow primary donors to have for the first time the data with which to make rational decisions about those budgets rather than simply guess about what is actually being done to serve their legitimate national interests or even the broader interests of the international community. The suspicion is that few UN programs and agencies would pass the test. Those that are found wanting and refuse to change or voluntarily go out of business should simply be starved of funds.

The secretary general . . . has estimated that perhaps half of the UN workforce does nothing useful.

We would lose very little by taking that step. Functional, highly specialized agencies such as the World Meteorological Association and the International Civil Aviation Organization, many of which predate the founding of the United Nations, would carry on pretty much as they always have. Useful diplomatic initiatives that the United Nations can do best could be preserved—provided that a corps of competent, and neutral, career diplomats can be recruited and retained. Peacekeeping missions would be limited to the relatively inexpensive monitoring arrangements that have worked over the years. Large-scale "peacemaking" operations, as attempted in Somalia and Bosnia, should be relegated to the wastebasket of failed experiments.

A vast overhaul

If the United Nations is to continue for another half century, more will be required than showering the institution with happy-talk birthday cards. The organization needs a vast overhaul of mission and method. In recent years the world body has been subjected to a variety of criticisms and suggested reforms. But the critiques rarely go far enough, and the remedies, particularly in the area of financial reform, would probably make matters worse rather than better. That is especially true of suggestions to give the United Nations even limited taxing authority.

The U.S. Congress can and probably will play a large leadership role in the campaign for either reform or abandonment. But the Congress cannot do it alone. The president has the solemn responsibility to take the lead in presenting the case for a continued U.S. interest in and support for an international organization that has been generously subsidized by American taxpayers yet has shown scant regard for their interests. UN personnel do not have jobs and budgets by divine right—although many act as if they do. Nor can their privilege of utter unaccountability be tolerated much longer.

A half century of experience with the United Nations should have resulted in a real review of its flaws. Instead, supporters of the organization frequently act as though it should be immune from criticism. Far more realism is required if the United Nations is ever to reach its centenary.

Greater realism may lead to the conclusion that the United Nations cannot be salvaged—or at least that the burden of doing so may exceed any prospective benefit. Strip away the sentimental, often self-serving rhetoric, the utopian and hence unachievable aspirations, and it may well be that the international body is no more relevant to the world's problems than the Holy Roman Empire was in its waning decades. If that is the case, we should rid ourselves of the United Nations as Napoleon did Europe of the empire in 1808.

Notes

1. See, for example, Thomas W. Lippman, "Florida GOP Freshman Moves to Scuttle the U.N.," *Washington Post*, November 6, 1995, p. A9, which outlines the views of Rep. Joe Scarborough (R-Fla.), who has introduced a bill calling for an end to U.S. membership in the United Nations after a four-year transition period. The congressman flatly denied that such a move was a retreat into isolationism, noting that he believed the United States would and should maintain its alliances with liberal democracies. For two recent suggestions for limited UN reform, see Inguar Carlsson, "The U.N. at 50: A Time to Reform," *Foreign Policy* 100 (Fall 1995): 3–18; and Ruben D. Mendez, "Paying for Peace and Development," *Foreign Policy* 100 (Fall 1995): 19–31.

2. Even the relatively successful operation in Mozambique demonstrated that various UN agencies are often shockingly incompetent. For example, the Office for Humanitarian Affairs Coordination managed to interfere with the work of other groups, which delayed unnecessarily the removal of land mines. See Tim Carrington, "Incompetence of the U.N. in Mozambique Casts Shadow over the Future of Haiti," *Wall Street Journal*, September 26, 1994, p. A10.

3. John R. Bolton, "A Good Year at the U.N.?" *Washington Post*, January 17, 1994, p. A23.

4. John F. Harris, "Clinton Calls on United Nations to Focus, Says It Must Trim Bureaucracy," *Washington Post*, June 27, 1995, p. A14. Other speakers included UN Secretary General Boutros Boutros-Ghali, Secretary of State Warren Christopher, and poet Maya Angelou.

5. Simon Duke, "The U.N. Finance Crisis: A History and Analysis," *International Relations*, August 1992, pp. 133–37.

6. Even if the United States had been a full league member (as it was Washington played a role behind the scenes), it is improbable that America would have sent troops to Spain or Ethiopia, marched into the Rhineland, prevented the Anschluss with Austria, or banged the tables at Munich in defense of Czechoslovakia. Given America's modest armed forces and the public fear of again being caught up in fighting foreign wars, the belief that such activism would have been forthcoming is based on wishful thinking, not logic.

7. According to article 16 of the league's covenant, "It is the duty of each member of the League to decide for himself whether a breach of the Covenant has been committed." Quoted in Hans J. Morgenthau, *Politics Among Nations: The Struggle for Power and Peace* (New York: Alfred A. Knopf, 1961), p. 304.

8. One mark of the Security Council's decline is apparent in this comparison: in 1948 the council met 168 times; a decade later the number of meetings had dropped to 36. Ibid., p. 485.

9. Ibid., pp. 489–90.

10. For a first-hand account of Kennedy's "profane" reaction to the neutrals'

moral cop-out at the Belgrade meeting, see Arthur M. Schlesinger Jr., *A Thousand Days: John F. Kennedy in the White House* (Boston: Houghton Mifflin, 1965), p. 520.

11. Julia Preston, "Massive World Body Resists Shaping Up," *Washington Post*, January 3, 1995, p. A1.

12. Ibid.

13. Duke, pp. 129–30.

14. Hans D'Orville and Dragoljub Najman, "A New System to Finance the United Nations," in *Security Dialogue* (Beverly Hills, Calif.: Sage Publications, 1994), pp. 136–37.

15. Duke, pp. 133–35.

16. Christopher S. Wren, "Mismanagement and Waste Erode U.N.'s Best Intentions," *New York Times*, June 23, 1995, p. A1.

17. Ibid.

18. Ibid. According to Wren, 1,500 of the 7,000 Secretariat personnel have no valid appointments. Those who have spent time in Third World government offices know exactly how that could happen; "employment" in such governments is often a very casual concept involving little or nothing in the way of a paper trail. For the total number of UN personnel, see Julia Preston, "U.N. Wrestles with Sexual Harassment in Its Ranks," *Washington Post*, September 8, 1994, p. A29; and Catherine Toups, "Peacekeeping Falloff May Lead to U.N. Cut," *Washington Times*, January 13, 1996, p. A10. See also William Branigin, "As U.N. Expands, So Do Its Problems," *Washington Post*, September 20, 1992, p. A1.

19. Karen Cheney, "It's the U.N.'s 50th Birthday, But Its Employees Get the Gifts," *Money*, November 1995, p. 27. The disparity in salaries is a long-standing problem. See General Accounting Office, "United Nations: Personnel Compensation and Pension Issues," Report to Congressional Requesters, February 1987.

20. Cheney.

21. See John M. Goshko, "U.N. Chief: Political Will, Money Needed," *Washington Post*, November 22, 1992, p. A1.

22. Richard Thornburgh, testimony, in *Management and Mismanagement at the United Nations: Hearing before the Subcommittee on International Security, International Organizations and Human Rights of the House Committee on Foreign Affairs*, 103d Cong., 1st sess., March 5, 1993 (Washington: Government Printing Office, 1993), p. 20.

23. Refet Kaplan, "U.N. Staff to Be Cut to Boost Efficiency," *Washington Times*, March 15, 1995, p. A1; and Preston, "Massive World Body Resists Shaping Up," p. A1.

24. Wren, "Mismanagement and Waste Erode U.N.'s Best Intentions," p. A1. His report goes on to note that $53,000 was requested for the 1994–95 UN budget for consultants' analysis of South African apartheid even though the country's first multiracial elections were held in April 1994.

25. James Avery Joyce, *Broken Star: The Story of the League of Nations (1919–1939)* (Swansea: Christopher Davies, 1978), pp. 78–79; and Jack C. Plano and Robert E. Riggs, *Forging World Order: The Politics of International Orga-*

nization (New York: Macmillan, 1967), pp. 22–23, 172–73. The league's Secretariat numbered about 600 and was drawn from 50 different nations. Yet the league's first secretary general, Sir Eric Drummond, a senior British civil servant, insisted that the Secretariat be recruited on an individual basis and that its members live up to the standards of the British civil service, then regarded as the world's most efficient.

26. Branigin, p. A1.

27. He was Martii Ahtisaari, at present Finland's president. Connor has had some small successes. His first budget proposal for 1996–97 is actually $109 million less than the previous one. He has selected some 200 jobs for elimination out of a Secretariat staff of more than 10,000. In UN terms, those are major accomplishments, but they hardly address the fundamental concern. See ibid. See also Julia Preston, "U.N. Chief Fires American in Charge of Reforming World Body," *Washington Post*, January 18, 1994, p. A20.

28. Richard Thornburgh, "Report to the Secretary General of the United Nations," March 1, 1993, reprinted in *Management and Mismanagement of the United Nations*, pp. 100–101. Thornburgh, at the request of President Bush, served one year as under secretary general in order to prepare the report on mismanagement at the United Nations.

29. Ibid., pp. 101–103.

30. Wren, "Mismanagement and Waste Erode U.N.'s Best Intentions," p. A1.

31. Catherine Toups, "U.N. Critics Call Report on Fraud a Prescription for Action," *Washington Times*, October 31, 1995, p. A13; and Christopher S. Wren, "Surprise! U.N. Auditors of Peacekeeping Missions Find Waste," *New York Times*, October 29, 1995, p. 18.

32. Catherine Toups, "U.N. Faces Increased Scrutiny at Age 50," *Washington Times*, June 26, 1995, p. A1.

33. Wren, "Surprise!"

34. Quoted in ibid. See also Toups, "U.N. Critics Call Report on Fraud a Prescription for Action," p. A13.

35. Quoted in Wren, "Surprise!" p. A18.

36. Catherine Toups, "U.N. Dues Proposal a Mixed Bag for U.S.," *Washington Times*, January 25, 1996, p. A1.

37. "Financing an Effective United Nations: A Report of the Independent Advisory Group on U.N. Financing," Ford Foundation, New York, April 1993, p. 26. On the current U.S. bill, see Catherine Toups, "U.N. Considers Imposing Taxes," *Washington Times*, January 16, 1996, p. A1.

38. The idea was first broached in 1994 in D'Orville and Najman, pp. 135–44. See also Mendez, p. 25.

39. Toups, "U.N. Critics Call Report on Fraud a Prescription for Action," p. A13.

40. "The United Nations Heads for Bankruptcy," *The Economist*, February 10, 1996, p. 41; and John M. Goshko, "To Help Ward Off Bankruptcy, U.N. May Lay Off More Than 1,000 Staff," *Washington Post*, February 3, 1996, p. A16. Apparently, some within the bureaucracy are getting the word as well. Rubens Ricopero, the new director of the UN Conference on Trade

and Development, is suggesting that his staff shrink by 10 percent. Perhaps. But UNCTAD for decades has been a steady advocate of the developed nations' transferring resources to the underdeveloped. Only lately have UNCTAD officials suggested that the private sector should have any input into the operations of the organization. In any case, any legitimate functions the UNCTAD may have acquired could be transferred to the World Trade Organization. Frances Williams, "UNCTAD Chief Pledges Sweeping Reforms," *Financial Times*, January 30, 1996, p. 5.

41. See remarks of Rep. Doug Bereuter (R-Neb.) on FAO corruption in *Management and Mismanagement at the United Nations*, p. 3.

42. Bolton.

43. Branigin, p. A1.

44. Anne Applebaum, "The U.N. Offers Summits, Not Solutions," *Wall Street Journal*, March 8, 1995, p. A20; and Preston, "Massive World Body Resists Shaping Up," p. A1. The Social Summit was the creation of Chile's ambassador to the United Nations, Juan Somavia, who lobbied Third World nations for their support of that dubious enterprise. Ibid.

45. Quoted in John M. Goshko, "U.N. Conferences Come under Fire," *Washington Post*, November 25, 1995, p. A16.

46. Branigin, p. A1.

2

The United States Should Force the United Nations to Reform

Jesse Helms

Jesse Helms is a Republican senator from North Carolina and chair of the Senate Committee on Foreign Relations.

The United Nations is in dire need of reform. Its bureaucracy has grown exponentially; its operating costs are too high; it is ineffective at resolving international conflicts; and it has overstepped its mission, threatening the sovereignty of nations. In order to force the U.N. to fix these problems, the United States should threaten to withdraw from the organization if reforms are not implemented. If reforms are not undertaken, the United States should in fact withdraw from the institution.

Not long ago, while accompanying U.N. Ambassador Madeleine Albright to an appearance in North Carolina, I was asked by a reporter whether the United States should withdraw from the United Nations. It was a valid question, to which I responded, "Not yet."

A quasi-sovereign entity

As it currently operates, the United Nations does not deserve continued American support. Its bureaucracy is proliferating, its costs are spiraling, and its mission is constantly expanding beyond its mandate—and beyond its capabilities. Worse, with the steady growth in the size and scope of its activities, the United Nations is being transformed from an institution of sovereign nations into a quasi-sovereign entity in itself. That transformation represents an obvious threat to U.S. national interests. Worst of all, it is a transformation that is being funded principally by American taxpayers. The United States contributes more than $3.5 billion every year to the U.N. system as a whole, making it the most generous benefactor of this power-hungry and dysfunctional organization.[1]

Jesse Helms, "Saving the U.N.: A Challenge to the Next Secretary-General," *Foreign Affairs*, September/October 1996. Reprinted by permission of *Foreign Affairs*. Copyright 1996 by the Council on Foreign Relations, Inc.

This situation is untenable. The United Nations needs to be radically overhauled. Yet Secretary-General Boutros Boutros-Ghali has ignored multiple warnings and stubbornly resisted reform that gets down to fundamentals. On the contrary, Boutros-Ghali has pursued a well-publicized campaign of what he calls U.N. "empowerment." He has protected the bloated bureaucracy, and the number and nature of peacekeeping operations has vastly expanded under his tenure. He has pressed for the establishment of a standing U.N. army and the power to collect direct U.N. taxes.

Now, with U.N. "empowerment" as his platform, Boutros-Ghali has reversed his pledge to serve a single term and is seeking a second one. The Clinton administration has belatedly announced its opposition but has failed to nominate or even search for a replacement, just as it has been complacent in the face of his presumptions to power.

The United Nations needs to be radically over-hauled.

Rather than Boutros-Ghali's "empowerment," the United Nations needs a stark reassessment of its mission and its mandate. The next secretary-general must help develop a bold plan to cut back the overgrown bureaucracy and limit its activities, then muster the political will and leadership to implement it. The reformist zeal of the next secretary-general will in all likelihood determine whether or not the United Nations survives into the next century. For if such a plan is not put forward and implemented, the next U.N. secretary-general could—and should—be the last.

Back to basics

The United Nations was originally created to help nation-states facilitate the peaceful resolution of international disputes. However, the United Nations has moved from facilitating diplomacy among nation-states to supplanting them altogether. The international elites running the United Nations look at the idea of the nation-state with disdain; they consider it a discredited notion of the past that has been superseded by the idea of the United Nations. In their view, the interests of nation-states are parochial and should give way to global interests. Nation-states, they believe, should recognize the primacy of these global interests and accede to the United Nations' sovereignty to pursue them.

Boutros-Ghali has said as much. In his 1992 *Agenda for Peace*, he declared his view that the sovereignty of nations is an outdated concept: "The time of absolute and exclusive sovereignty . . . has passed. Its theory was never matched by reality. It is the task of leaders of states to understand this." In other words, U.N. member nations, including the United States, should be willing to abandon claims of "absolute and exclusive sovereignty" and empower the United Nations by ceding it a measure of their sovereignty. They should give the secretary-general a standing army and the power to collect taxes—functions that legitimately rest only with sovereign states.

Such thinking is in step with the nearly global movement toward greater centralization of political power in the hands of elites at the expense of individuals and their local representatives. In the United States, Europe, and elsewhere, political leaders are belatedly recognizing the destructive effects of central bureaucracies and state-controlled economic activities and are fighting uphill battles to bring these into check. They are finding, however, that once established, bureaucracies (along with the goodies they dispense) are nearly impossible to dismantle. This virus of centralization is spreading to the global level, and the United Nations is its carrier. Just as massive bureaucracies have taken hold in Europe and the United States, the U.N. bureaucracy has established a foothold on the international stage.

This process must be stopped. In the United States, Congress has begun a process of devolution, taking power away from the federal government and returning it to the states. This must be replicated at the international level. Reining in the U.N. bureaucracy goes hand in hand with Congress' domestic agenda of devolution. U.N. reform is about much more than saving money. It is about preventing unelected bureaucrats from acquiring ever-greater powers at the expense of elected national leaders. It is about restoring the legitimacy of the nation-state.

The United Nations needs a stark reassessment of its mission and its mandate.

How big is the problem? According to the latest official U.N. statistics, the organization is home to 53,744 bureaucrats, comprising the Secretariat bureaucracy and those of the diverse specialized agencies. Hard as it is to believe, some advocates of the United Nations argue that it is not big enough. In his book *Divided It Stands: Can the United Nations Work?* James Holtje writes that "when one considers that . . . [the United Nations is] expected to meet the needs of 5.5 billion people worldwide, the number begins to look small." It is not the job of the United Nations to "meet the needs" of 5.5 billion people—that is the job of nation-states.

But the U.N. bureaucracy mistakenly believes that caring for the needs of all the world's people is exactly its job. From the bureaucracy's vantage point, there are no international, national, or even local problems—all problems are U.N. problems. Thus we have the recent Habitat II conference in Istanbul, where the United Nations spent millions of dollars to address the concerns of cities—an issue that legitimately should be handled by local or national governments.

So what is wrong with the United Nations lending a helping hand on these matters? The issue is not just sticking the U.N.'s nose where it does not belong. By making every problem its problem, the United Nations often makes the situation worse. Instead of helping nation-states solve problems, the United Nations does the exact opposite—it creates a disincentive for states to handle problems that are their responsibility to resolve. When every local or regional problem becomes a global one, the buck stops nowhere. Solving it becomes everyone's responsibility, and thus no one's responsibility.

The war in Bosnia is a perfect example. Dealing with Serbia's illegal aggression and genocide in Bosnia was the responsibility of the European powers, in whose region the crisis lay, and of the United States, which considers itself a European power. But instead of addressing the issue themselves, the Clinton administration and our European allies pushed responsibility for handling this problem onto the United Nations, which accepted a mission it was incapable of fulfilling. The U.N. peacekeeping operation became an excuse for inaction by the Europeans and Americans, who used the United Nations to pretend they were addressing the problem. As a result, thousands upon thousands of innocent civilians died, while the United Nations, through a combination of impotence and negligence, did nothing to stop the genocide.

The United Nations also complicates matters by giving states with no interest in a particular problem an excuse to meddle without putting anything concrete on the table. Countries that have no natural interest in an issue suddenly want to get involved, and the United Nations gives them the legitimacy to do so without cash or constructive contributions. What, for example, are countries like Togo, Zaire, Panama, or Ireland, or China for that matter, prepared to contribute to bringing about Middle East peace? They have no legitimate role in the peace process, save that which their U.N. membership (and in some cases seats on the Security Council) gives them. What the United Nations ends up doing is giving lots of countries a seat at the table who bring nothing to the table.

By making every issue a global issue, the United Nations is attempting to create a world that does not exist. A United Nations that can recognize its limitations—helping sovereign states work together where appropriate and staying out of issues where it has no legitimate role—is worth keeping; a United Nations that insists on imposing its utopian vision on states begs for dismantlement.

Goals of reform

Successful reform would achieve the twin goals of arresting U.N. encroachment on the sovereignty of nation-states while harnessing a dramatically downsized United Nations to help sovereign nations cope with some cross-border problems. Such reform must begin by replacing Boutros Boutros-Ghali with a new secretary-general who will go in on day one with a daring agenda to reduce bureaucracy, limit missions, and refine objectives.

Second, there must be at least a 50 percent cut in the entire U.N. bureaucracy. The Clinton administration has made the standard of reform a "zero-growth" budget. This is inadequate. So long as this bureaucracy remains in place, it will continue to find new missions to justify its existence.

Third, there must be a termination of unnecessary committees and conferences. Since its founding as an organization of five organs in 1945, literally hundreds of U.N. agencies, commissions, committees, and subcommittees have proliferated. Today, for example, the United Nations includes a Committee on Peaceful Uses of Outer Space, which counts among its crowning achievements the passage of a resolution calling upon sovereign nations to report all contacts with extraterrestrial beings directly to the secretary-general.

In addition to massive, wasteful conferences like the Beijing women's summit and Habitat II, the United Nations continually sponsors work-shops, expert consultations, technical consultations, and panel discus-sions, in 1995 some 7,000 in Geneva alone. Most of these can be termi-nated at a savings of millions of dollars.

Fourth, the U.N. budgeting process must be radically overhauled. Budgets for U.N. voluntary organizations are currently amassed through a bidding process, where nation-states must make capital investments prior to involvement in specific issues or projects under U.N. auspices. This should be the model for the entire U.N. budgeting system. The secretary-general currently has a budget of roughly $1 billion to pay for the activities of the Security Council, General Assembly, Economic and Social Council, Secretariat, and International Court of Justice, plus the ad-ministrative costs of numerous relief, development, and humanitarian agencies. This budget is voted on by the General Assembly, where the United States has no veto, and where every nation—whether democratic or dictatorial, no matter how much or how little it contributes to the United Nations—has an equal vote.

This system should be abolished. Instead, the secretary-general should be limited to a bare-bones budget of some $250 million, and U.N. activities should be funded on a voluntary basis. This would essentially subject all U.N. programs to a market test. Each country would decide the value of programs by how much they were willing to pay. Those pro-grams that are really vital will continue to receive support, while those championed only by the bureaucracy will die of malnutrition.

The United Nations has moved from facilitating diplomacy among nation-states to supplanting them altogether.

Some bargaining will naturally result (country X would say to country Y, you help with my project, and I'll help with yours). But this system would dramatically cut down on waste, eliminate freeloaders, empower member states vis-à-vis the bureaucracy in budget determinations, give states a voice in the U.N. commensurate with their willingness to pay while forcing wealthier countries to pay more, and give the United States and others the option not to fund or participate in programs they are currently compelled to support, but which they feel directly violate their interests.

Lastly, peacekeeping must be overhauled. Peacekeeping is the United Nations' fastest-growing industry. In 1988, the total cost of U.N. peace-keeping operations around the world was just $230 million; in 1994, it was $3.6 billion. Of that, the United States was directly assessed nearly $1.2 billion, plus additional in-kind contributions of personnel, equip-ment, and other support totaling roughly $1.7 billion (all of which was skimmed off the U.S. defense budget).

Not only have costs proliferated—so has the scope of peacekeeping missions. Prior to 1990, most peacekeeping missions were just that: mon-itoring truces, policing cease-fires, and serving as a buffer between parties. Today, however, peacekeeping has evolved into a term without meaning. It is used to justify all sorts of U.N. activities—everything from holding elections to feeding hungry people to nation-building. As the system now works, the United States has two choices: go along with a proposed peace-keeping operation and pay 31.7 percent of the cost, or veto the mission, which we do not like to do. The system should permit a third option: al-low the United States to let missions go forward without U.S. funding or participation. If others in the world want to undertake nation-building operations, there is no reason the United States should discourage them—so long as American taxpayers do not have to pay for a third of it. This would allow the United Nations to serve the purpose it was designed for: helping sovereign states coordinate collective action where the will for such action exists. And, of course, Security Council members would re-tain the authority to veto missions they deem wholly inappropriate.

Forcing change

The time has come for the United States to deliver an ultimatum: Either the United Nations reforms, quickly and dramatically, or the United States will end its participation. For too long, the Clinton administration has paid lip service to the idea of U.N. reform, without imposing any real costs for U.N. failure to do so. I am convinced that without the threat of Amer-ican withdrawal, nothing will change. Withholding U.S. contributions has not worked. In 1986, Congress passed the Kassebaum-Solomon bill, which said to the United Nations in clear and unmistakable terms, reform or die. That did not work. A decade later, the United Nations has neither reformed nor died. The time has come for it to do one or the other.

Legislation has been introduced in the House of Representatives by Rep. Joe Scarborough (R-Fla.) for the United States to withdraw from the United Nations and replace it with a league of democracies. This idea has merit. If the United Nations is not clearly on the path of real reform well before the year 2000, then I believe the United States should withdraw. We must not enter the new millennium with the current U.N. structure in place. The United States has a responsibility to lay out what is wrong with the United Nations, what the benchmarks for adequate reform are, and what steps we are willing to take if those benchmarks are not met by a certain date.

The United Nations will certainly resist any and all reform—particu-larly many of the smaller and less developed members, which benefit from the current system and gain influence by selling their sovereignty to the organization. That is why the next secretary-general has an enormous job to do: his or her mandate will be nothing less than to save the United Nations from itself, prove that it is not impervious to reform, and show that it can be downsized, brought under control, and harnessed to con-tribute to the security needs of the 21st century. This is a gargantuan, and perhaps impossible, task. But if it cannot be done, then the United Na-tions is not worth saving. And if it is not done, I, for one, will be leading the charge for U.S. withdrawal.

Note

1. There is no single entry in the U.S. budget for contributions to the United Nations. Ambassador Charles Lichenstein, a former U.S. representative to the United Nations, has calculated the $3.5 billion figure thus: the U.S. share of

the U.N. administrative budget, $298 million; the U.S. share of the U.N. peacekeeping budget, $1.2 billion; U.S. contributions to all U.N. specialized agencies, $368 million, excluding capital contributions to the World Bank and the International Monetary Fund; the value of goods and services the United States voluntarily contributes toward U.N. peacekeeping and the U.N. system as a whole, $1.7 billion to $2.0 billion. In recent years Congress has withheld a fraction of this amount as pressure for U.N. reform.

3

The United Nations Should Reduce Its Military Role

Jim Wurst

Jim Wurst is a journalist based at the United Nations and the editor of Disarmament Times.

In 1992, the secretary-general of the United Nations issued a report outlining an expanded, militaristic role for U.N. peacekeeping forces. U.N. operations in Bosnia and Somalia, which were both failures, resulted from policy changes brought about by that report. The United Nations should retreat from these military-style operations and concentrate on diplomatic and humanitarian efforts.

The United Nations began its 50th year [1995] by reflecting on the wreckage of its experiments in policing the new world order, then taking a deep breath and learning the art of the possible. Secretary-General Boutros Boutros-Ghali began the year with a report to the Security Council on the third anniversary of his "Agenda for Peace," the report that set the stage for the peacekeeping trajectory.

The unimaginatively titled report, "Supplement to an Agenda for Peace," does not directly say the UN has erred; to do so would mean Boutros-Ghali would have to admit to mistakes. His record shows this doesn't come easily. But he did make a few digs at the Security Council, such as accusing it of micro-managing peacekeeping missions. This led US Ambassador Madeleine Albright to remark that, at least in assessing blame, the report "was a bit off the mark," adding "I think we have to guard against saying that every time there is a success, it is due to the United Nations, and every time there is a failure, it is due to the member states."

Pulling back from peacekeeping

Squabbling aside, the real significance of the report is its suggestion that the UN should pull back from its ambitious agenda in peacekeeping. Boutros-Ghali clearly envisages fewer Bosnia-type operations and greater emphasis on non-military initiatives such as mediating and rebuilding societies after wars end. Though he wrote that better enforcement capacity

Jim Wurst, "Downsizing the Peace Agenda," *Toward Freedom*, March 1995. Reprinted by permission of *Toward Freedom*, 209 College St., Burlington, VT 05401; subscriptions, $25/year.

is desirable in the long term, he also claimed that "it would be folly to attempt to do so at the present time when the [UN] is resource-starved and hard pressed to handle the less demanding peacemaking and peacekeeping entrusted to it."

The UN has swung between extremes, from trying to accomplish too much (Somalia) to doing too little (Rwanda). It has dangerously blurred the line between peacekeeping (working to stabilize a truce) and peace enforcement (the current jargon for fighting), as well as the line between military and humanitarian actions. Coming close to admitting a mistake, Boutros-Ghali noted, "Nothing is more dangerous for a peacekeeping operation than to ask it to use force when its existing composition, armament, logistic support and deployment deny it the capacity to do so." The firewall between military and humanitarian missions has crumbled so badly, it's nearly impossible to remember that the UN force in Bosnia is officially a humanitarian mission.

The reasons why

With so much attention focused on the continuing disaster in Bosnia, it isn't immediately obvious that peacekeeping missions are decreasing. After massive growth in operations in 1992–93, including notorious missions in Somalia and Bosnia and successful ones in Cambodia and El Salvador, the number remained steady in 1994 at 17, with little change in costs and number of personnel. In the first quarter of 1995, three missions (all successful) wound down. The few operations on the horizon are small.

Among the main reasons for this downsizing: the SG and secretariat are coming to grips with their limitations; member states talk a good game but in the end won't commit money or personnel; and the types of war the UN has handled poorly are disappearing.

The firewall between military and humanitarian missions has crumbled so badly, it's nearly impossible to remember that the UN force in Bosnia is officially a humanitarian mission.

This last point shouldn't be interpreted as suggesting that war is fading away. But the kinds of war that have been so destructive, both for local victims and the UN, were born from the end of the Cold War (or in the case of southern Africa, the end of apartheid's ruthless destabilization campaigns). Those conflicts are winding down. The new ones are mostly internal: nine out of the eleven UN peacekeeping missions established [between 1992 and 1995] were intra-state conflicts. Nearly all of the storm clouds on the horizon are also internal.

Peacekeeping 1995

There is one area of expansive innovation where UN ambitions haven't stretched beyond its capabilities. Integrated civilian and military operations to help solidify a peace agreement and rebuild a country have worked when the Security Council provided adequate resources and all (or most) of the warring parties accept UN involvement. The 1989–90 mission in Namibia was ambitious and successful. Subsequent operations in Cambodia, El Salvador and Mozambique also must go into the plus column.

Haiti will be the next important test of the UN's capacity to handle complex operations. It has the elements for success and failure: a realistic mandate for restoring peace, a country sunk so low there's no bottom left, a population that wants the UN to help restore order, a hostile elite with enough guns and money to subvert any peace plan, a major outside power (the US) perfectly willing and able to wreck any developments that don't go its way. The UN's shameful acquiescence in Washington's power games in 1993–94 could be redeemed by an honorable effort to help Haitians control their fate. Or Haiti could become Bosnia in the Caribbean.

A testing ground for the small-scale will be—get out your maps!—Tajikistan. One of the smallest Central Asian nations born out of the demise of the Soviet Union, Tajikistan has been entangled in civil and external wars since independence. In September 1994, a cease-fire was negotiated, and in December the Security Council created a modest 40-person observer/mediation mission. Although the cease-fire is holding, the situation is tense, marked by deep division among the Tajiks and an abundance of powerful outsiders fiddling about, including Russia, Iran and Afghanistan.

It will take much more than 40 observers to keep the peace. But if progress can be made toward reconciliation, and if the UN plays a constructive role in that process, then it may be on its way toward learning the fine art of the possible.

Meanwhile at headquarters, the secretariat has developed some innovations. These include more and regular consultations with troop-contributing countries. Since these countries have a very direct stake in the safe operation of a mission, they can inject a needed dose of reality. Other new ideas are better coordination between the Department for Humanitarian Affairs and relief agencies, both UN (such as UNICEF and the World Food Program) and independents; and weekly high-level coordination meetings for the Departments for Political Affairs, Humanitarian Affairs and Peacekeeping.

Besides improving in-house coordination, these new procedures have the effect of increasing civilian input over peacekeeping. One of the reasons why the UN drifted into more military actions was the relative absence of civilian influence to counter the instinctive reach for the gun. Now that it has proven itself incapable of launching military operations, mediators and humanitarians have a chance to prove that the institution still does have a role in the new world.

4

The United Nations Is a Threat to U.S. Sovereignty

Thomas A. Burzynski

Thomas A. Burzynski is a researcher at the New American *magazine in Appleton, Wisconsin.*

The U.N.'s International Covenant on Civil and Political Rights was ratified by the United States in 1992. This document threatens American sovereignty and undermines the U.S. Constitution by allowing the U.N. to interfere in the domestic affairs of the United States. In an attempt to implement the covenant, the U.N. has falsely accused the United States of violating the human rights of prisoners and has criticized America's system of government and its Second Amendment protection of the right to bear arms. In order to eliminate the threat that the covenant poses, the United States must withdraw from the U.N. and force the organization to leave the country.

> Police brutality was rife, the Government was powerless to intervene and people needed to be protected from torture. In addition, prisoners in jails were subject to cruel and degrading treatment. Immigrants and refugees too were often held in indefinite detention and, in general, those groups were subject to human rights abuses.
>
> —United Nations Press Release, February 1995

You might think that the above UN summary describes cruel and inhuman conditions existing under the oppressive regimes in Red China, former Yugoslavia, Iraq, or some other wretched locale. But instead, the press release is a paraphrase of remarks made by Juliet Spohn-Twomey of the World Council of Churches before the UN Human Rights Commission, and the cruel conditions she was describing supposedly exist in—the United States.

In March 1995 a U.S. government delegation obediently presented itself before the stern, displeased UN Human Rights Committee, an affiliated body of the Human Rights Commission, to defend the U.S. government's

Thomas A. Burzynski, "U.S. on U.N. Carpet," *New American*, May 15, 1995. Reprinted with permission of the *New American*.

record on human rights and to answer questions on the issues brought up by Spohn-Twomey. The U.S. delegation, led by John Shattuck, Assistant Secretary of State for Democracy, Human Rights, and Labor, and Deval Patrick, Assistant Attorney General for Civil Rights, appeared before the 18-member committee to give a progress report on our nation's implementation of the UN's International Covenant on Civil and Political Rights.

A giant step backward

The UN covenant, written in 1966, was not ratified by the U.S. until 1992, but, like all UN agencies, resolutions, and actions, has rarely been implemented or enforced without U.S. backing and funding. The covenant itself poses dangers to all aspects of American life. During Senate hearings on ratification, Senator Jesse Helms (R-NC) argued that the "covenant calls into question the right to freedom of speech, and freedom of the press, and just punishments . . . and even the federal/state structure of our legal system. . . . This covenant, in sum, is a step backward into authoritarianism. . . ." Unlike our own form of government, which is based on the truth that people get their rights from God, the Covenant on Civil and Political Rights is based on the idea that the world body itself can establish, and thus nullify, rights.

This is demonstrated in Article 19 of the covenant, which declares (on UN authority) that "everyone shall have the right to freedom of expression . . . subject to certain restrictions." Those restrictions, of course, are to be determined on a case-by-case basis by an unaccountable UN bureaucracy.

The UN Human Rights Committee was authorized by this same covenant, which requires that all signatories submit reports "whenever the Committee so requests." The current Human Rights Committee is composed of "experts" from such bastions of freedom as Egypt, Ecuador, and India. These committee members dutifully chastised the U.S. for its various alleged human rights abuses. Defenders of the UN might argue that the U.S. is represented on the committee. And, we are. The U.S. representative is Thomas Buergenthal, former UNESCO official and Fulbright professor on human rights and current member of the Council on Foreign Relations.

> *The UN would, no doubt, find it easier to influence and control the U.S. government and its citizens if all the power were deposited in one national government.*

The committee questioned the U.S. delegation on a wide range of domestic topics, such as the treatment of Native Americans (Indians), women, prisoners, minorities, immigrants, and refugees. Other issues included statehood for the District of Columbia, police brutality, and executions of juveniles convicted of capital crimes after being waived into adult court. The committee expressed collective dismay that federal and state prisoners might be kept for extended periods of time in jail cells with no windows. Also discussed were the rights of residents of DC in comparison with residents of the 50 states. The racial makeup of inmates on death row even came up in the session. All of this from the UN, an organization which states in Article I, Section I of its own charter that its primary purpose is "to maintain international peace and security. . . ." The committee's concerns should come as no surprise: In 1992, Senator Helms predicted that "these countries . . . will use U.S. ratification [of the covenant] to make false charges of violations" of human rights abuses in this country.

A threat to the Republic

One of the more alarming topics reviewed by the UN committee concerns our nation's federal system of government. According to a UN report, committee members expressed some doubts that the UN covenant could be effectively implemented under a system that gives so much independence to states. Committee member Rajsoomer Lallah of Mauritius said that states "must determine how they would implement the obligations which had been undertaken on behalf of their country." Cecilia Medina Quiroga of Chile cautioned that state laws must be under "continuous review." Andreas Mavrommatis from Cyprus cited differences among states in their protection of homosexuals as evidence of the "disparity" between federal and state governments.

Fausto Pocar of Italy asked what steps were being taken to bring state laws into line with the covenant. Pocar admitted that the question of state compliance was an internal matter of the United States. The UN would, no doubt, find it easier to influence and control the U.S. government and its citizens if all the power were deposited in one national government rather than dispersed among 50 states and a federal government. Through our federal system, some protection from this Godless and un-American covenant is given to U.S. citizens. Nonetheless, American citizens and their federal system of government were betrayed by the ratification of this document: Article 50 of the covenant clearly requires that the "provisions of the present Covenant shall extend to all parts of federal States without any limitations or exceptions."

In line with the UN's drive to disarm all countries and citizens, committee members voiced distress over the Second Amendment to the Constitution. A UN press release summarized Andreas Mavrommatis of Cyprus as opining that the "covenant did not prohibit the bearing of arms but imposed a duty on the Government to protect life. One of the means to protect life was to prohibit or control the use of firearms." The delegate from Japan, Nisuke Ando, argued that the covenant contains "an implicit assumption that the right to life should not be jeopardized, either by public authority or by private hands."

By far the biggest concern of the Human Rights Committee was the "failure" of the U.S. to make the covenant part of domestic law. When the Senate ratified the covenant it attached certain reservations which made it non-binding on U.S. courts. However, those reservations could easily be removed by the Senate, which would cause UN law to be woven into the fabric of American society and would allow courts and citizens to employ the covenant directly against UN "scofflaws."

Committee member Eckart Klein of Germany suggested that the U.S. presented a false "Constitution-centric" view that all the rights in the covenant were represented in U.S. law. The delegate from Ecuador observed (correctly) that the U.S. move represented a "limitation" on the covenant, and Omran El-Shafei of Egypt warned that the failure of the U.S. to fully embrace the covenant could provide an excuse for other countries to abandon the covenant.

The UN has long desired for countries to absorb its resolutions and treaties into their domestic law. Such a move is critical to world government. The world witnessed in the Gulf War what could happen if a country rejects or ignores a UN resolution.

Progressive implementation

The United States delegation responded to the various criticisms and concerns of the Human Rights Committee with submission. Assistant Secretary of State John Shattuck conceded that "our system is not perfect" and that the United States represented a "work in progress." Shattuck spoke, in essence, of further corrupting the U.S. Constitution by progressively implementing the covenant into the U.S. system. One method for doing this was explained by Conrad Harper, legal adviser to the Department of State. Harper told the UN committee that all 50 state attorneys-general had received a copy of the covenant so that they could work to ensure state compliance. Copies were also sent to the 50 state bar associations. A more indirect method of preparing for total implementation of the covenant came out in a remark by John Shattuck, who noted that the covenant was already being used in some human rights courses on college campuses and in law schools.

> *Only our nation's complete withdrawal from the UN and removal of the United Nations from American soil will destroy this threat to our precious liberties.*

To what end would UN advocates in the U.S. work towards progressively implementing the International Covenant on Civil and Political Rights? One clue might come from the example of Argentina, whose recent past includes military juntas, riots, and accusations of human rights abuses much like those made against the U.S. by Juliet Spohn-Twomey. According to a March 1995 UN press release, an Argentine delegation recently appeared before the Human Rights Committee and declared that in Argentina, "international human rights treaties [have] a standing higher than all other Argentine law and [are] equal to the Constitution itself. . . ." According to an Argentine official, the country's newly drafted 1994 constitution, along with UN covenants, would now safeguard human rights and help Argentina get past "our own sad events." A Human Rights Committee briefing paraphrased Thomas Buergenthal, the U.S. member on the UN committee, as saying that Argentina's new constitution is "revolutionary in what it [seeks] to achieve and should serve as a model for other countries."

Should the U.S. cave in to the UN via pressure from such kangaroo courts as the UN Human Rights Committee, perhaps it will not be long before our own laws are "harmonized" to conform with those of the United Nations. Certainly it is only through the steadfast efforts of such lawmakers as Jesse Helms that we have not already arrived at that place.

It will take the courage of all good Americans to guarantee that our beloved Republic does not get sucked down the sewer of the United Nations' Godless new world order. Only our nation's complete withdrawal from the UN and removal of the United Nations from American soil will destroy this threat to our precious liberties.

5

The United States Should Withdraw from the United Nations

Andrea Seastrand

Andrea Seastrand is a Republican congresswoman from California.

Since the end of World War II, American foreign policy has been heavily influenced by the United Nations. U.S. involvement in costly foreign entanglements in Korea, Vietnam, and Bosnia were the direct result of America's ties to the international organiza- tion. In order to preserve U.S. sovereignty and prevent the squan- dering of American money and lives, the United States should withdraw from the United Nations.

For nearly 50 years the United Nations has been the hub around which U.S. foreign policy has revolved. This entangling alliance with the world body and its web of specialized agencies and institutions has re- sulted in our involvement in one foreign quarrel after another, from Ko- rea to Vietnam to Bosnia. We have paid dearly, in terms of blood, treasure and potential loss of sovereignty, for ignoring the sound advice of our first president, who stated in his farewell address: "The great rule of con- duct for us, in regard to foreign nations, is, in extending our commercial relations, to have with them as little political connection as possible."

Increasing human suffering

In such recent trouble spots as Rwanda, Somalia and Bosnia, the U.N. has not merely proved inept in reducing conflict and human suffering; its ef- forts have served to increase both. In Bosnia, U.N. policy from the begin- ning bolstered the Serbians at the expense of the Bosnian Muslims. The arms embargo, which effectively hamstrung only the Muslims, is merely one indication of that effect. Sadly, U.S. policy under the previous Re- publican and current Democrat administrations has let the deplorable U.N. policy lead us by the nose.

Andrea Seastrand, "Is It Time to Consider U.S. Withdrawal from the United Nations? Yes: U.S. Security and World Peace Would Benefit from a Pullback," *Insight*, August 28, 1995. Reprinted with permission from *Insight*. Copyright 1995 by The Washington Times Corporation.

A political cartoon showed the Bosnian Serbs and the Muslims in a boxing ring. As the Serbs repeatedly delivered punishing left hooks, jabs and right crosses to the head of the Muslims, Uncle Sam stood behind the Muslims and held their arms back. That is what we did with this dreadful U.N.'s policy. Not only could the Muslims not launch an offensive combination of punches to regain a fair position in the fight, they could not even bring their arms up to defend against the barrage launched against them.

Congress worked to undo the damage caused by the Bosnian arms embargo. The Senate, by a veto-proof margin, voted to lift the arms embargo to allow the Muslims to defend themselves and the House voted to do the same. If this president will not lead in foreign policy, Congress will serve as a means to make basic, sound decisions regarding our world leadership.

A sow's ear

Virtually everyone appears to agree that the U.N. is plagued with serious defects. The question is whether such flaws can be mended through reform or are so deeply embedded that the time has come for the United States to withdraw rather than waste time in a futile attempt to make a proverbial silk purse out of what from its inception was a sow's ear. For instance, while professing adoration for "democracy," the U.N. is one of the least-representative political entities in the world. The concept of one-nation, one-vote has sanctified minority rule within the organization, and there is no realistic way to change it under the supermajority requirements for amending the U.N. charter.

In the 185-member U.N. General Assembly, the United States, with nearly 262 million citizens, has the same vote as Palau, the U.N.'s most recent member, with a 1990 population of slightly more than 15,000. Ten other nations have populations less than 75,000. One hundred two countries, with a combined population less than that of the United States, compose a 55 percent majority in the General Assembly, while 166 nations (90 percent) have a combined gross domestic product that is less than that of the United States.

In such recent trouble spots as Rwanda, Somalia and Bosnia, the U.N. has not merely proved inept in reducing conflict and human suffering; its efforts have served to increase both.

This imbalance has its most serious impact when the vast majority of small and poor nations join together to approve policies related to war, economic expenditures, wealth redistribution and regulatory restrictions that only the minority of prosperous countries can finance and conduct.

There appears to be a built-in orientation toward waste and extravagance, as there is with most large government bureaucracies. For instance, in response to the man-made famine and resulting human suffering inflicted on Ethiopia by dictator Mengistu Haile Mariam in the eighties, the General Assembly's Fifth (Administrative and Budget) Committee voted to designate $73.5 million in U.N. funds for Ethiopia. But the money was earmarked not to feed the starving but to embellish conference facilities of the U.N.'s Economic Commission for Africa in Addis Ababa. In response to criticism, a U.N. spokesman vigorously argued that the upgraded facilities were sorely needed because "the support facilities at Africa Hall are wholly inadequate for the needs of the ECA." The diet of the average Ethiopian also was wholly inadequate at the time. The American taxpayers' share of the U.N.'s facelift was $18.4 million.

It may come as a surprise to the average American taxpayer that U.S. citizens employed by the U.N. do not, in essence, pay income tax. Their tax burden is reimbursed in full by the U.N. The reason, as explained by the State Department, is to assure that all U.N. employees "have equal take-home pay for equal work." Since the United States picks up a quarter of the U.N. tab, it means that most taxpayers are subsidizing the lucky few who work for the world body. For 50 years the U.N. has depended largely on "contributions" from member states to finance its activities, but now there are increasing calls for imposition of a tax (or taxes) that would provide reliable and substantially increased funds.

Absolute power

One can only cringe at the prospect of a United Nations empowered with legislative, executive and judicial powers backed by a global military, regulatory and taxing apparatus. Such power would be the most absolute that the world has ever seen.

At the U.N.'s founding 50 years ago and for a few years thereafter, it was claimed that the organization was "mankind's last, best hope for peace." Today, Americans increasingly recognize that the U.N. has sponsored wars, passed one-sided resolutions (the arms embargo against Bosnia) and imposed a selective standard of justice.

There are those who maintain that despite the many drawbacks associated with our involvement in the U.N., we should stay in the organization to promote the good accomplished by some of its specialized agencies. Actually, if we were to withdraw from (and stop financing) the General Assembly and Security Council, we still could support whatever specialized agencies we wish. The first order of business is to decide whether we should dissolve our financial and political ties to the Security Council and General Assembly, a move largely unrelated to what we then do about the specialized U.N. agencies.

Virtually everyone appears to agree that the U.N. is plagued with serious defects.

The matter of human rights is another issue on which the United Nations' view is intrinsically at odds with the traditional American view. The first article of our Bill of Rights, for instance, states that "Congress shall make no law respecting an establishment of religion, or prohibiting the free exercise thereof; or abridging the freedom of speech, of the press, or the right of the people peaceably to assemble, and to petition the Government for a redress of grievances." That wording clearly protects speech, reporting and petitioning that criticizes government. But consider the Universal Declaration of Human Rights, the U.N.'s basic human-rights standard the General Assembly approved unanimously in 1948. The declaration espouses numerous rights in its early articles, then neuters them with this startling proclamation in Article 29, paragraph 3: "These rights and freedoms may in no case be exercised contrary to the purposes and principles of the United Nations." Which would seem to mean that the article you are reading could be banned, as could any other effort critical of the alleged purposes and principles of the United Nations.

Replacing the U.N.

If the U.N. were to be dismantled, with what would it be replaced? Author G. Edward Griffin, who has written extensively on U.N.-related issues, suggests that we try freedom, by which he means "freedom for all people, everywhere, to live as they please with no super-government directing them; freedom to succeed or to fail and to try again; freedom to make mistakes and even to be foolish in the eyes of others." Griffin contends that "until all nations follow the concept of limited government, it is unlikely that universal peace will ever be attained."

Someone once speculated that peace on Earth would come when its peoples had as much as possible to do with each other, and their governments had as little as possible to do with the lives of the people. Most Americans likely would support a federation of nations that was honestly intended to increase the freedom of individuals, goods and cultures legally to cross national boundaries and to decrease government restrictions on individuals. But the United Nations has, since its founding, been a powerful force pushing in the opposite direction.

Americans increasingly recognize that the U.N. has sponsored wars, passed one-sided resolutions . . . and imposed a selective standard of justice.

There has never been a friend of the free-enterprise economic system at the U.N.'s helm. Those who have held the post of secretary-general since the U.N. was conceived have favored big, rather than limited, government. The list includes the current secretary-general, Boutros Boutros-Ghali of Egypt, who has sought dramatically to strengthen the U.N. militarily while emphasizing wealth redistribution as an economic solution to the plight of poor nations.

The U.N.'s heavy emphasis on wealth redistribution appears to be immune to meaningful reform. If the U.N. and its specialized agencies were allowed to confiscate everything from the "have" countries and distribute it to peoples in the "have not" nations, the overall misery of the latter would scarcely be affected. There are simply too many of the latter, thanks in large part to the oppressive collectivist governments under which they live. If those countries could break free of the shackles of socialism that weight them and adopt the basic economic principles that were largely responsible for our own abundance, the contribution to world stability and well-being would be unprecedented. The United Nations, sadly, stands as a roadblock to such a change. It must be removed before there will be a real chance to cope effectively with the problems of world hunger and poverty.

Former U.S. Ambassador to NATO Harlan Cleveland observed in the mid-1960s that "it is almost impossible even to think about a durable world peace without the United Nations." Today, it seems even more inconceivable to contemplate a durable world peace while the U.N. meddles. As the noted American journalist Henry J. Taylor once wrote, U.N. diplomacy "is like a man walking in the woods who stopped when he saw a snake. It turned out to be a stick. But the stick he picked up to kill it with turned out to be a snake." Throughout its 50-year existence the U.N. has proved to be more serpent than savior. In the 1970s former New Hampshire Gov. Meldrom Thomson concluded his overview of the U.N. in his book, *Live Free or Die*, with these words: "Let us, withdraw from the United Nations and insist that the United Nations withdraw from the United States." Today, that conclusion needs to be seriously discussed, debated and then acted upon in this country whose role as world leader is in question when we defer to the often ludicrous decisions of the United Nations.

In the words of Margaret Thatcher, "Consensus is the negation of leadership." If we continue to make our foreign policy subservient to the will of the U.N., we will risk forfeiting our position as moral world leader.

6

The United Nations Should Be Disbanded

Richard Gott

Richard Gott is literary editor of the Guardian, *a British newspaper.*

Many people had hoped that the United Nations would become a relevant force in the wake of the cold war. Since then, however, the U.N. has increasingly been attacked as being a corrupt, wasteful, and ineffective organization. In fact, in its current form, the U.N. is a conservative organization that serves the interests of capitalist countries, and it is incapable of being reformed as a democratic institution. As public support continues to subside, the U.N. is likely to implode—and its demise should not be mourned.

The United Nations, forever bumbling away in the background, has been so much part of our lives for the past half century that it is difficult to imagine the time when it won't be there any more. Yet all the evidence suggests its days are numbered.

A sustained attack

Many people hoped that the UN would rise phoenix-like from the ashes of the Cold War, but these early hopes have clearly not been fulfilled. Today its very existence is in doubt. As its activities in former Yugoslavia, Somalia and Cambodia have been closely scrutinized, the UN has come under sustained attack—from press and politicians and the public. It is not perceived as 'our' UN any longer, but as someone else's, and 'those people', whoever they may be, are now endlessly portrayed as corrupt and incompetent.

Overstretched and underfunded, bureaucratically and unimaginatively organized, the UN is perceived to straddle the globe like a dinosaur, fed only by the pious hopes of those (now rather elderly) people who once dreamed that it could be used to forge a better world; and by those time-serving diplomats created in each other's image who make up what is sometimes almost laughingly referred to as 'the international commu-

Richard Gott, "Death of a Dinosaur," *New Internationalist*, December 1994. Copyright 1994 by New Internationalist. Reprinted with permission.

49

nity'. From Sarajevo to Phnom Penh, from Nicosia to San Salvador, the UN's thin blue line of 'peacekeeping forces' is uncertainly deployed, confused participants in a global strategy that has lost all historical validity and over which no group or sentient individual seems to have adequate control.

Given the head of steam that is building up against it, it seems likely that the UN, like the League of Nations before it, will have vanished into history by the end of the century. The programmes put forward for its reform, most recently the American suggestion that Germany and Japan should be admitted to the Security Council, are not signs of life but symptoms of its decline.

A couple of years ago I spent some months in New York with the purpose of examining the activities of the Security Council and the General Assembly at close quarters. Travelling there with the usual set of historically acquired assumptions common to the liberal left, I was prepared to believe that the UN was an interesting and potentially progressive institution with a new lease of life. Though traditionally under the control of the great powers, there was a clear possibility that, with the end of the Cold War, it might enjoy some new flexibility of manoeuvre.

No reform is possible

I returned with a somewhat different set of beliefs that have become hardened over time. Today's UN is an intrinsically conservative institution, operating almost solely for the benefit of the advanced capitalist world. It is no longer capable of reform along progressive lines, particularly after the collapse of the Soviet Union and the Third World.

Public support for the UN in Western countries is now conspicuous by its absence and this will prove eventually to be its Achilles' heel. An isolationist President in the US, with the Americans concentrating on internal affairs and the breakdown of their own country, will have neither the time nor the inclination to manipulate the UN. Without active American support the organization will implode.

We have got used to thinking of 'the West' as a coherent and cohesive unit, yet this era is clearly drawing to a close. The G7 countries may soon fall out among themselves. The US itself may never again take a leadership role. We spend so much time extrapolating existing trends—particularly in the ecological debate—that we often forget our political parameters can suddenly change, just as they have since 1989.

The UN—with its all-embracing centralist ambitions—is a dangerous anachronism.

To understand what is happening we need now to go back in history and ask ourselves why we have supported such an extraordinary concept as a world organization at all. The great international organizations we have known in this century—the League of Nations and the UN—have always been assemblies of colonial powers designed essentially to prevent inter-imperial conflict. That has been the pattern and it is difficult to see how it could be changed.

The General Assembly of the UN is not, and could never be, a democratic organization. If it were, the world would be run by the Chinese. One has only to look at the difficulties of organizing a United Europe to realize that a United World would be a wholly utopian venture. Public opinion in the West is utterly unprepared to accept losing its soldiers in foreign wars that it is in no way geared to comprehend.

So I believe now that we should rid ourselves of any residual enthusiasm for the UN; we should regard it with the same kind of suspicion that was once reserved by the Left for the CIA or any other institution that seeks to protect the privileges of the status quo powers. We should shed no tears if it were to disappear.

In the philosophically post-modern world in which we are now regrettably forced to live, the UN—with its all-embracing centralist ambitions—is a dangerous anachronism.

7

The United Nations Can Play an Important Role in World Peacekeeping

Lincoln P. Bloomfield

Lincoln P. Bloomfield is professor of political science emeritus at the Massachusetts Institute of Technology. He has served in the U.S. Navy, in the State Department, and on the National Security Council.

After the breakup of the Soviet Union, it seemed that the United Nations would be pivotal in reducing cross-border conflicts much like the one in Iraq and Kuwait in the early 1990s. Instead, most of the recent violent conflict is occurring within national boundaries. The world has a responsibility to intervene to end this intrastate violence, and the United Nations should play a large role in this endeavor. The U.N. should focus its efforts on preventing the ethnic violence and other forms of conflict that threaten world stability.

In the five years from 1945 to 1950 a monumental victory was won over tyranny, a major new challenge loomed, the democracies responded with strategies for the long haul, and a whole set of international institutions was set in motion to perform important pieces of the world's business.

In the five years from 1989 to 1994 a monumental victory was won over tyranny, new challenges loomed, the United Nations (UN) began to cope with them, the democracies were overcome in varying measure by self-absorption, moral flabbiness, and military vacillation, and the prospects were shaken for the kind of reformed international security regime their interests dictate.

How could that happen? What kind of international security system is realistically possible? What should be the U.S. role in such a regime?

Post-communist surprises

Reversing Iraq's assault on Kuwait in 1991 seemed to jump-start the process of collective security. But cross-border aggression was not the

Lincoln P. Bloomfield, "The Premature Burial of Global Law and Order: Looking Beyond the Three Cases from Hell," *Washington Quarterly*, vol. 17, no. 3, Summer 1994, pp. 145-61; ©1994 by the Center for Strategic and International Studies (CSIS) and the Massachusetts Institute of Technology.

main challenge of the 1990s. Instead, the volcano of change spewed forth what Václav Havel called "a lava of post-communist surprises," generating a panorama of turbulence and strategic ambiguity as multinational states broke up, and other states simply broke. For leftover conflicts UN peacekeeping was the method of choice to monitor cease-fires and help with transitions in old cold war battlefields from Angola and Mozambique to El Salvador and Nicaragua, along with older trouble spots like the Western Sahara, Namibia, Suez, southern Lebanon, and Cyprus.

The trickiest of the new threats arose not among states and their surrogates, but from mayhem within state borders.

But the trickiest of the new threats arose not among states and their surrogates, but from mayhem within state borders. Renewed anarchy in Cambodia, man-made starvation in Somalia, mugging of newly won democracy in Haiti, and slow-motion genocide in Bosnia all violated not so much the "law" as the underlying moral order. It was behavior that article 2 (7) of the UN Charter bars the organization from touching because it is "essentially within the domestic jurisdiction of any state." Those new cases would also not have passed the cold war test of "strategic threat." But with the fear of superpower escalation gone, and with a potent assist from worldwide TV coverage, they powerfully assailed the conscience of the nations. Waiting in the wings were equally hairy scenarios of tribal warfare in Russia's "Near Abroad" [countries that were formerly republics of the Soviet Union] and in some "states-but-not-nations" like Burundi, along with human rights outrages in Sudan, Myanmar, Iran, Syria, the People's Republic of China—you name it.

Working within a drastically altered strategic landscape, a born-again UN Security Council began a chapter of law-in-the-making with novel interventionary doctrines to deal with famine-producing anarchy, ethnic cleansing, and the deliberate creation of refugees. It was not exactly "peacekeeping" as in Cyprus, and certainly not "collective security" as in the Persian Gulf. It was an unprecedented "policing" function carrying such provisional labels as "peacemaking," "humanitarian enforcement," and "second-generation operations," led by a United States committed to a stance of "assertive multilateralism." The UN Charter's criterion of "threats to the maintenance of international peace and security" became stretched beyond recognition. But despite all the ambiguities, the early 1990s looked like an open moment for the liberal internationalists' dream of a system of global law and order, and one equipped with a heart. The moment was brief.

Three cases from hell

The new era of multilateral intervention for humanitarian purposes began fairly successfully in Iraq after the defeated regime turned savagely on its disaffected Kurdish population in the North. In response to public outrage, the victorious coalition moved inside Iraqi territory and established protected aid channels to "Kurdistan," although not in the South where the regime was busily crushing Shi'ite dissidence. Successive UN resolutions mandated destruction of long-range ballistic missiles and weapons of mass destruction, along with unprecedentedly intrusive monitoring of missile testing and other sites. When Baghdad boggled at monitoring, UN threats backed by U.S. bombing of selected targets alternated with promises to unfreeze badly needed Iraqi oil revenues, and in February 1994 the International Atomic Energy Agency (IAEA) reported that all declared stocks of weapons-grade material had been shipped out. But compliance by Baghdad came only after credible threats of punishment. Indeed, these events also raise the question of whether an offending power has to be militarily defeated before the community will *enforce* its norms against intolerable national behavior.

Three other UN "peace-enforcement" operations did not pose that particular question but for other reasons brought the trend to a screeching halt. In Somalia, where anarchy was generating mass starvation, the UN was shamed into action by Secretary General Boutros Boutros-Ghali, and the Security Council for the first time launched a peacekeeping operation not requested by the "host government" (in this case there was no government at all). Humanitarian aid was authorized with a mandate to create "a secure environment" for its delivery. The primarily U.S. force used both diplomacy and military presence to stem the famine, but the UN mission became controversial when it actually used force to create the required environment. Willingness to back up a humanitarian operation with force if necessary may turn out to be the price of humanitarian intervention by the international community. But the reaction of risk-averse Americans to casualties fewer than New York experiences in a slow week suggests that the use of force, even to carry out a unanimously agreed mission, had better remain as a last resort, particularly if the situation on the ground gets murky—as it invariably does.

Events also raise the question of whether an offending power has to be militarily defeated before the community will enforce *its norms against intolerable national behavior.*

In splintered former Yugoslavia, the UN undertook another humanitarian mission of aid to refugees, in an environment in which Serb authorities escalated their noxious policy of "ethnic cleansing" to uproot and terrorize Bosnian Muslims. The Security Council authorized use of "all means necessary" to protect aid. But Britain and France, which had put a modest number of noncombatant peacekeepers on the ground, balked at facing down those blocking aid. In May 1993 the Council established six "safe havens" for embattled Muslim populations and authorized force to protect, not the people, but the peacekeepers. But once more the available enforcers of the community's rules were unwilling to stand up for their own norms.

It was only after a particularly murderous—and televised—mortaring of a Sarajevo market crowd that the North Atlantic Treaty Organization

(NATO) finally stirred itself into a credible posture and Serb guns were pulled back. Nothing could more clearly illustrate both the "CNN effect" and the painful truth that bullies respond only to believable threats. But it was disgracefully late in coming and useless to the thousands already left dead and the hundreds of thousands left homeless.

In Haiti the issue was restoration of democratic rule in the face of official thuggery. To do so required at least a believable show of force. But a United States once burned wanted none of that and executed a humiliating retreat, leaving the Security Council incapable of enforcing its own decisions. (The equally involved Organization of American States [OAS], faithfully reflecting Latin America's deep resistance to anything resembling intervention, was not a credible alternative.)

In diplomacy as in war, success has 100 fathers but defeat—or even plain bad luck—is an orphan. In Bosnia a European Union suffering from tired blood and historical amnesia for far too long turned away from its responsibilities, and Washington—regrettably but in my view correctly—declined to act alone. In Somalia and Haiti humanitarian intervention was overtaken by a bloody endgame between claimants for power. In all three cases the Security Council and secretary general made some questionable judgments, and the responsible powers blinked when it came to taking casualties. Just when the international community had begun to act like one, its staying power and seriousness of purpose were suddenly in serious question.

Defining U.S. interests

Debate about the future world role of the United States soon became hostage to the three "cases from hell." An administration without a settled strategy shared its internal uncertainties with a Congress that smelled blood in the water. Indispensable public support, already weakened by erratic leadership, was not edified by news media that tend to portray all events as random, and public confusion echoed back to a government that often bases policy on opinion polls. Pessimism replaced post–Cold War euphoria as a shortlist of foreign situations of minimal strategic importance distorted the already complex process of redefining U.S. economic and political interests.

To regain its balance, the United States badly needs a coherent strategy toward the changed nature of conflict. To create one requires that present difficulties be assessed in the light of broad national interests. So far this has not really happened, and the great sucking noise one hears is the sound of fragments of doctrine rushing to fill the conceptual vacuum. Utopian internationalists keep themselves marginalized without a strategic perspective, while leftover strategists still misunderstand the power of global issues. Single themes like "new world order," "end of history," "clash of civilizations," have been attention-getting but are, like all sound bites, too simplistic. Isolationism as a policy is absurd, but the United States cannot and will not play the role of global policeman.

How then can a workable basis be found for policy toward the internal implosions and struggles that dominate our times? In February 1994 President Bill Clinton belatedly asserted U.S. national interests toward Bosnia.[1] But a rational longer-term policy will be based on three more fundamental national interests.

One primordial interest is the worldwide economic position of the United States, which requires at least minimal political stability around the shrunken globe.[2] U.S. global interests are negatively affected by any turbulence that threatens to create a dangerous whirlpool in the stream of international relationships. Global economic and other interests simply cannot be satisfied with a laissez-faire policy toward conflict.

A second interest grows out of the 200-year preference of Americans to show a benign and humane external face to the world. (By a curious coincidence, George Washington's farewell address embodies a similar dual prescription.) Cooperative attempts to maintain international "law and order" used to be entirely optional. Given the unprecedented role of TV, the growing role of whistle-blowing private groups, and the extraordinarily consistent public opinion favoring UN peacekeeping,[3] it is a delusion to think that demands for human rights or political justice can now be dismissed as a sideshow the United States can avoid at will.

The third fundamental U.S. interest is the most problematic. It stems from core values of political democracy and free enterprise, summarized in the Clinton administration's commitment to "enlargement of democracy." Haiti was seen by some as a test of this interest, and there will doubtless be others as feeble new democracies come under strain. But this policy will encounter the 200-year-old argument between active U.S. proselytizing versus simply keeping, in Henry Clay's words, "the lamp burning brightly on this western shore, as a light to all nations." History also suggests that democracies keep the peace better than tyrannies, and where a recognizable democratic process is throttled by its enemies—Grenada was an even clearer case than Haiti—it ought to engage U.S. interests.

The policy objective flowing from those interests is not complicated. It is to achieve a threshold level of "law and order" in the international community that enhances U.S. global purposes as well as embodying a fundamental concern for conflict limitation and, yes, justice. The wrong question to ask is "Should the United States be the world's policeman?" Even if a president sought that role, it would not long be tolerated by other countries, not to mention Congress and the American people. If the United States will not support forceful intervention in situations that do not obviously threaten its "vital" interests, the rational alternative is a far more focused effort to *prevent* conflicts, which I will come to shortly. The central questions then are: "How is the international community, global or regional, to deal with situations of destabilizing anarchy, clandestine weapons programs, or gross political criminality that exceed the bounds of tolerability on strategic or humanitarian grounds?" and "What role should the United States play in that quest?"

Is there really an "international community"?

Discussions of multilateralism assume the existence of an "international community," but some challenge that concept as a figment of the liberal imagination. In a little-remarked assertion in a much-discussed article Samuel Huntington stated that "the very phrase 'the world community' has become the euphemistic collective noun . . . to give global legitimacy to actions reflecting the interests of the United States and other Western powers."[4] Is he right? How different from a genuine community is today's international society?

According to political theory, a viable community rests on a minimum consensus of community-held values. It is endowed with core powers of taxation and policing, which depend on a relative monopoly of force. People generally accept rules because of a shared sense of commonality, whether ethnic, linguistic, religious, or ideological. They also benefit from a governance system that protects them from physical threats. People know what "compliance" and "enforcement" mean in familiar local settings. They know the cost of breaking the rules and consider believable the probability of enforcement action, whether by cops on the beat, sheriffs, tax-collectors, or armies.

Government works because there is a presumptive self-interest in abiding by the rules and a known penalty for noncompliance. Is international society today capable of behaving like a real rather than a rhetorical community, armed with enforceable "law and order" rules complete with credible incentives to comply and disincentives to misbehavior? The answer is "No—but."

Isolationism as a policy is absurd, but the United States cannot and will not play the role of global policeman.

When it comes to bottom-line law and order, the limiting realities are the world's infinite variety, decentralized power centers, fragmentary structures, and primary reliance on self-help with only a contingent possibility of community "police" assistance when threatened. The combined logic of economic interdependence, technology, and weaponry tells us that peace, security, and prosperity all require strengthened forms of "international governance."[5] But international society is still a bit like 1930s China, equipped with a "constitution" and functioning central apparatus, but with real power monopolized by provincial warlords, some benign and cooperative with the center, some decidedly not. The UN may simulate a government; but it cannot really act like one. World society is a partial and imperfect community when it comes to gut qualities of sovereignty, legitimacy, and power. Its characteristics all fall short of the definition of true community.

But does that really mean that all recent actions in the international system can be explained by U.S. pressure? Hardly. Enormous majorities in the UN voted to condemn the Iranian seizure of the U.S. embassy in 1979. Why? Because states of every religion and ethnic background have a deep interest in keeping inviolate the global diplomatic nexus. Large majorities condemned the Soviet invasion of Afghanistan in 1979 and the Iraqi invasion of Kuwait in 1991. Why? Because virtually all agree on the primordial rule of interstate relations that forbids invading, trashing, and obliterating the identity of a neighboring state. Thousands of troops from 57 non-Western countries help to staff 18 current UN operations in the field. Why? Because they decided their national interests are served by that kind of community policing.

At the UN Conference on Environment and Development in Rio in 1992 the great majority—opposed, incidentally, by the United States— voted goals and policies reflecting the conclusions of cross-cultural environmentalists. And over 140 states have voluntarily signed the Nuclear Non-Proliferation Treaty (NPT). Why? Because sensible people have noticed the twin realities of environmental interdependence and the unusability of nuclear weapons.

Even in the most neuralgic sector, UN human rights bodies have recently distanced themselves from their ideological and cultural biases and now publicize violations in Muslim, Orthodox, Christian, Slav, Turkic, Jewish, and secular societies—including the United States. One reason has been Western pressure to apply what are arguably universal values. But equally influential is the revolution in mass communication that informs people about common standards of civility.

The evidence is obviously mixed, and several things are going on at once. But there are unmistakable signs that some broad common values and interests are cutting across "civilizations." It is this evidence of commonality that constitutes the foundation of a minimal "world community" for limited but crucial common purposes. To turn Marx on his head, the basic global *structure* is composed of states and significant nongovernments, powerfully driven by their cultures. Common problems none can handle alone constitute the agenda of the *superstructure* of agencies of international cooperation and coordination. The global architecture is, so to speak, split-level, and one level is not going to replace the other.

So is there a genuine "world community"? Not really. Should we act as though it exists on matters of common concern? Of course. The goal is certainly not world government, which even if practical could become world tyranny. But the system already functions effectively in the sectors where states agree to pool sovereignty without actually saying so. Indeed, the UN's critics do not challenge (or even seem to know about) the networks that already monitor and to a degree regulate global trade, telecommunications, mail, health, air travel, weather forecasting, nuclear power, and refugee flows.

The UN may simulate a government; but it cannot really act like one.

Most of the powers of governance will continue to be "reserved" to the member states on the model of the U.S. Constitution, and we should not become distracted by theological arguments about sovereignty. The vexing question as we grope our way toward the next stage of history is how to achieve improved compliance with the limited but crucial rules agreed upon by the larger community.

Here, of course, is the central dilemma of the "international community." In a true community the actions required to cope with violations of its rules add up to a graduated continuum of responses—a kind of updated "escalation ladder," based on the principle that the earlier one achieves compliance, the cheaper and less hair-raising the level of policing required. But in a world of sovereign states the center has no independent power, national interests change, today's terrorists and war criminals can become tomorrow's rulers, the UN inherits conflicts after they have got out of hand, ground rules are imprecise, aggression has never been universally defined, threats to peace are subjectively assessed, and ethnic cleansing and making refugees of one's own people are not adequately on the lawbooks.

The times are not propitious for upgrading the enforcement of international "law and order" beyond some useful but modest procedural fixes.

This is not to say that nothing can be done now to improve matters. UN supporters have proposed new varieties of stand-by forces, whether old-fashioned "chapter 6½" peacekeeping units in blue berets, "chapter 6¾" peacemaking/peace-building protectors in flak jackets, or even a standing 10,000-man "UN Legion."[6] The end of the Cold War also revived discussion of the never-implemented article 43 agreements under which the great powers would make major forces available to the Security Council. Secretary General Boutros-Ghali's *Agenda for Peace* is a major, if premature, statement of both doctrine and plans for what he terms "peace enforcement."[7]

Some practical operational processes can also be reformed, such as headquarters operations, which need to be more efficient, and the UN information system, which is improved but still needs to be more autonomous and to have backup from national intelligence (as it reportedly had in Iraq from the U.S. Central Intelligence Agency and Britain's MI5). It is at least theoretically possible that such improved readiness would make it easier to respond to calls for UN intervention.

Proposals for improved "law and order" functions must also deal with other security sectors that raise similar questions of predictability and coherence in international—and U.S.—responses, most critically the violation of rules barring proliferation of weapons of mass destruction. North Korea's 1993 announcement that it was dropping out of the NPT inspection system pressed a hot button. A combination of threats and inducements to secure international inspection of suspected nuclear sites was improvised by the United States acting de facto for the NPT and UN community. The IAEA can turn as a last resort to the Security Council, but nothing is said about what happens next. (The same is true for other potential international crimes for which compliance arrangements are still embryonic—state-backed terrorism against civilian targets, international drug trafficking, electronic sabotage of transnational networks, illicit traffic in nuclear or toxic wastes, perhaps ultimately criminality in the "global commons" of outer space and the deep sea bed.)

Counterproliferation policy runs up against two special obstacles. First, the barn door is partly open, thanks to clandestine bomb-building by Israel, India, and South Africa (before it turned back) and potentially by Pakistan, Iraq, North Korea, and Brazil. Second, it will always be argued—and it will always be true—that such arrangements are inherently discriminatory, leaving weapons and technologies of mass destruction in

U.S., European, Russian, and Chinese hands and keeping others from their assumed benefits.

Common sense kept some countries from going nuclear, and the stigma of second-class membership can still be alleviated by attractive "carrots" and by including have-nots at the decision-making tables.[8] The line generally held during three decades, even as some famous scientists, along with President John F. Kennedy, confidently predicted at least 30 nuclear weapons powers by 1970 or 1980. And it is true that the current collection of treaty cheaters—Iraq, Iran, North Korea—constitutes an exceptional, small category of states committed to destabilizing the neighborhood, which is generally not the aim of those who already possess the offending capabilities.

Counterproliferation will feature ambiguities as ambitious states find the threat to go nuclear more bankable than crossing the threshold.[9] But some clandestine weaponeering may appear so threatening that states will decide not to wait for the stately processes of what Harlan Cleveland calls a "committee-of-sovereigns-with-a-staff." The Israeli air force engaged in do-it-yourself enforcement in 1981 to abort progress in Iraq's Osirak reactor, and in extremis such "unilateral enforcement" may have to be repeated. U.S. policy correctly assigns a high priority to counterproliferation, and if all else fails the United States may have to trade off higher later costs by risking a confrontation with an isolated North Korea.

A modest midterm scenario

The times are not propitious for upgrading the enforcement of international "law and order" beyond some useful but modest procedural fixes, but the issue is of course far more political than it is technical. Action is always subject to veto by the permanent members of the Security Council, and Russian and Chinese cooperation cannot be taken for granted in perpetuity. Nevertheless, conditions may return that make progress again possible, and it is useful to have a defined goal in mind as a target for discussion and planning. The following sketches a modestly reformed process that falls short of what happens in cohesive communities, but goes beyond what most people consider feasible today.

A more coherent international system will feature compliance procedures that resemble a process of *law enforcement*. It will look less like a traditional binary choice between war or peace and more like a step process that mimics domestic *policing*. Violations of agreed rules will take many forms along a broad continuum, matched by a continuum of community responses.

A state-backed bomb-thrower or electronic terrorist represents the lowest end of the law-breaking spectrum. Next come violations involving limited nuclear, chemical, biological, or missilery development, all potentially reversible. A more serious challenge comes from a pair of countries threatening or sporadically skirmishing against each other. And a major threshold is crossed when organized, uniformed military forces engage in "small wars." A similar threshold is crossed with an internal "small war" when civil strife afflicts the global conscience or imperils regional stability. At the extreme end lie the wars of conquest of other peoples' countries.

A step process of "community responses" begins with article 33 of the Charter, which enjoins states to settle disputes themselves before unloading them on the UN. Early-stage responses are exemplified by the diplomat with the briefcase and the observer with the binoculars and electronic sensors. At the next step up, failure to halt illicit work on weapons would bring a kind of SWAT team of technicians such as IAEA inspectors accompanied by UN guards in civvies (as in Iraq today) armed with state-of-the-art nonlethal weapons.[10] If fighting breaks out but can be halted, the truce would, as now, be monitored by nationally contributed, nonfighting, peacekeeping units—a low-cost trip wire, primarily symbolic but respected because the sides want to be separated, whatever their rhetoric.

Coercive enforcement starts with article 41 economic and communications sanctions. For the first 40 years international sanctions were applied only twice—on Rhodesia (ineffectively) and against South Africa (military only, but more effective because observed by the major powers). Recent UN sanctions against Iraq, Haiti, and Serbia were technically effective, those against Libya and Angola less so. But sanctions against Iraq, Haiti, and Serbia devastated the innocent. Sanctions should be targeted primarily on leaders' overseas bank accounts and travel rights, and compensation should be made to third countries that suffer from sanctions the way Turkey did in the Iraq case.

If diplomacy and peacekeeping fail, a well-armed blue-bereted "posse" would use whatever force is required to persuade the sides to separate and get relief supplies to civilians—the still unlabeled "peacekeeping plus" model of armed humanitarian intervention that for so long tragically failed on this count in Bosnia. As discussed below, the compliance force could be drawn from one already in existence such as NATO, an invigorated regional organization such as the OAS or the Organization of African Unity (OAU), or a future Asia-Pacific security organization.

A more coherent international system will feature compliance procedures that resemble a process of law enforcement.

The greatest need up to this point on the spectrum is for technical personnel who can monitor, recognize, and if necessary dismantle illicit weaponry and production; for "peace officers" on the lines of U.S. marshals, who can protect both relief operations and UN monitors; and for quick-reaction U.S. National Guard–type units that can be dispatched to protect the protectors—precisely the capabilities that never successfully functioned in the cases from hell.

The final point is the rare instance of coercive military force under article 42—son of Desert Storm, as it were. Overt armed aggression is mercifully rare. But we have learned the hard way that some few situations turn out to be genuinely nonnegotiable, and that doctrinal pacifism can give a green light to aggression and tyranny, whether to a Hitler planning the conquest of Europe, a Saddam Hussein coveting neighboring states, or Serbs and Croats murderously pursuing dreams of expansion. All act in the spirit of Bismarck who, asked if he wanted war, reportedly said "Certainly not, what I want is victory."

If the community leaves matters until this explosive point, it will confront the worst case: having to force compliance with Security Council directives through deployment by powerful states of UN-flagged national ships, tanks, and assault helicopters, whether under article 43 or not. If the aggressor is a nuclear-armed great power, the system will be back where it was at the height of the Cold War. As discussed shortly, this is one of many persuasive reasons to focus on conflict prevention.

A role for regional organizations?

So far the reference point has been the UN Security Council. Given overload at the global center, calls are once more heard to "beef up" regional and subregional organizations so they can carry more of the burden of peacekeeping and perhaps even armed "peacemaking." Chapter VIII of the UN Charter flags regional organizations as the first port of call for dispute settlement, and some modest successes have been scored in this realm. But until now they have proved poor "law and order" agents for the community, either because a major regional country was battling the rest (Cuba in Latin America, Israel in the Middle East, South Africa in Africa) or because, as with NATO, the purpose of the organizations was something different. All these situations have changed and greater reliance on regional organizations is consistent with the larger trend toward decentralization of functions in both public and private sectors. They will, however, have to change significantly if they are to share the peacemaker's burden. Assuming that such changes are at least theoretically possible, what would a modestly improved system look like?

In Latin America, under the Bogota Pact and Rio treaty, the OAS is equipped, at least on paper, with a wide spectrum of functions ranging from conflict resolution to collective security. It has had modest success in fact-finding and dispute settlement, as have subregional groupings such as the Contadora Group in Central America. OAS peacekeepers served in the Dominican Republic (following U.S. intervention), but the organization has been notably allergic to anything resembling intervention by its own members (and to U.S. domination). Freed of Cold War hang-ups that entangled the United States in Cuba, Nicaragua, and El Salvador, the OAS would take the lead in actively policing the region. The OAS would become the primary regional peace-keeper, with the Security Council invoked only in exceptional circumstances. Considering Latin America's oversize military establishments as well as the U.S. military's role in mentoring what turned out to be some of the region's most obnoxious military figures, regional military training would focus on peacekeeping units for ready deployment at the call of the OAS, much as Scandinavia has trained its splendid peacekeepers.

Much the same applies to the African region—not tomorrow but perhaps the day after. The OAU has played a role in a few regional situations and actually sent peacekeepers to Chad in 1981, but it has been irrelevant to most African conflicts. Individual countries have sometimes acted as subregional cop, for instance Tanzania in Uganda. Ethiopia's leaders have played an impressive role in trying to bring peace to Somalia, and a regional military force from the Economic Community of West African States worked hard to overcome anarchy in Liberia. In November 1993 the OAU secretary general announced tentative agreement on a mechanism for conflict management and a fund for such operations. With that kind of capability, the OAU could replace the UN (and the United States) for further policing duties in Somalia and take the lead in Burundi and in other regional outbreaks of anarchy, genocide, or famine. On any political calculus, subsidizing the proposed African fund would be more cost-effective for the West than direct involvement.

It is too early to envisage a midterm regional peacemaking role in the Asia-Pacific region, which is in the early stages of organization, and where the United States will have to act as strategic makeweight for some years to come. But in Europe a dual NATO role of deterrence and peace enforcement, prefigured in Bosnia in February 1994, could serve several important purposes.

As the world's premier military alliance, NATO should be a prime source for regional peacekeeping and regional peace enforcement (and has indeed already offered to do just that). NATO—that is to say, its members—failed its first important test in that department when it refused until tragically late in the day to use even a fraction of its incomparable military power to protect the delivery of humanitarian aid—or its own peacekeepers—in former Yugoslavia. Prudence dictates that NATO also retain its historic mission aimed at deterring any would-be hegemonic Eurasian power (implicitly Russia, with Germany again as subtext). As new uncertainties increase the pressure for inclusion of Central European states, it will be important to declare a genuinely dual role for NATO. Russia unilaterally—and helpfully—dealt itself into the peacekeeping game in Bosnia. It should be explicitly made a senior partner in regional peacekeeping missions to offset any new paranoia about encirclement—and to preempt any Russian imperial moves via "unilateral peacekeeping." NATO should be explicitly reconstituted a regional organization under chapter VIII of the UN Charter, its membership expanded, and its secondary mission clarified as the primary maintainer of peace and security in the Eurasian region.

Some who prefer an all-Europe team argue that the European Community (now Union), through the incorporeal Western European Union (also absent from Bosnia), should become the future peacekeeper of choice in the region. Others look to the not quite so incorporeal Conference on Security and Cooperation in Europe (CSCE). Like NATO, CSCE has agreed to supply peacekeeping troops to the UN, and in fact maintains an observer mission in Macedonia. But it had to withdraw its observers from Kosovo, 10 of its 52 members are involved in shooting wars, and it has no real power.

Making preventive diplomacy a reality

If U.S. global interests require a generally stable external environment, and if the present UN and existing regional organizations cannot at this time consider expanding their police function to deal with destabilizing disorder and intolerable national behavior, and if the United States declines to be the global policeman, what is the alternative?

The question answers itself. The best available strategy is to head off violations before they take place. This is true whether the offender is a ruler contemplating a territorial grab, a pair of countries deadlocked over a disputed border, a rogue political force like the Khmer Rouge threatening to sabotage an international agreement, a majority regime abusing a minority, or a resentful people smarting under an unjust treaty. "Conflict prevention" and "preventive diplomacy" are now much in vogue. The challenge is to transform them from slogan to policy.[11]

In fact the record of quiet diplomacy to defuse potential crises is far from zero, often featuring unsung heroes whose triumphs are rarely trumpeted. Nor does one have to go further than chapter VI of the UN Charter to discover the comprehensive battery of devices available for resolving or moderating disputes before they become small wars. Even a modest revival of the 1920s vogue of compulsory arbitration treaties would be an improvement, and some have reappeared on the scene. But in the main, modern history is a dismal chronicle of missed opportunities to take effective preventive steps, followed by later painful costs.

The best available strategy is to head off violations before they take place.

No collective preventive/deterrent efforts were seriously undertaken prior to the war between Britain and Argentina over the Falkland Islands (Malvinas), or the buildup leading to Iraq's invasion of Iran in September 1980. In the Gulf, the application of purposeful disincentives by Washington and London, instead of self-deception and wishful thinking, might have brought about a different outcome. The glaring example of too little and too late is former Yugoslavia, where Germany insisted on premature recognition of Catholic Croatia and Slovenia, Washington reportedly discouraged an early compromise agreement to partition Bosnia,[12] and European politicians declined to counter unspeakable behavior on their own doorstep.

What, in concrete terms, can be done to strengthen preventive diplomacy? Three available approaches are publicity, deterrence, and proactive peaceful change procedures.

Publicity. In the age of global communications, publicity has already become a powerful diplomatic instrument, with the international spotlight a proven tool for noncoercive compliance through its powers of, so to speak, shame, embarrassment, and ridicule. Governments are resistant to open discussion of alleged misbehavior, official candor concerning which can be downright embarrassing. But intense commercial television coverage stimulated action in Ethiopia, Somalia, and eventually Bosnia, and there is now a UN high commissioner for human rights with modest powers of inquiry and reporting. It continues to be important for Amnesty International and other nongovernmental human rights groups to throw a healthy glare on egregious behavior regardless of governmental nervousness. And so that network news editors do not always set the action agenda, every UN observer mission should carry its own camcorder, with the UN making the videotapes available at cost.

Much recent attention has been devoted to crisis prevention centers and other techniques for diplomatic early warning. Such procedures can be useful, if only to force attention to incipient hot spots governments know about but would prefer to ignore.[13] But even with ample warning, the management of current crises invariably takes priority over longer-range planning or prophylactic diplomacy. Whistle-blowing does not always deter and is not always followed by action. What else might help?

Deterrence. Given its crucial importance for more general conflict prevention, deterrence should not remain the conceptual monopoly of nuclear strategists. Some modern disasters might have been averted by a credible and timely threat of sanctions for noncompliance by incipient aggressors, abusers, and proliferators. Conflict-prevention military units can be stationed on a threatened border before fighting breaks out (as is taking place on the Macedonian side of the Serbian-Macedonian border— but not along the preinvasion Iraq-Kuwait border). More forcefully, if the European powers (or the United States) had moved early to confront the latter-day vandals off Dubrovnik, or to actively protect relief supplies and UN peacekeepers at Sarajevo airport when first fired upon, or had consistently punished violations of their no-fly zone, things might have turned out differently. Even later, if the huffing and puffing in major Western capitals had added up to a credible threat, the radical Balkan expansionists might have been stopped earlier. But Serb and Croat leaders soon understood that the threats were hollow, and remained undeterred until the carnage was virtually completed. The policy prescription is embarrassingly obvious: democratic leaders should follow through on their threats to enforce the "law," or undemocratic ones will make fools and hypocrites of them.

Some modern disasters might have been averted by a credible and timely threat of sanctions for noncompliance by incipient aggressors, abusers, and proliferators.

Deterrence is one of the reasons to codify meaningful sanctions against human rights abuses. U.S. legislation has denied some aid to egregious violators, and occasionally reforms have followed (with due acknowledgment of the logical fallacy of *post hoc, ergo propter hoc*). But the community's rulebook needs a sharper set of teeth. The UN Genocide Convention, along with the Fourth Geneva Convention and its successors on laws of war, should be expanded to cover "slow-motion genocide" of the Yugoslav variety. Sanctions should be added to the declaration on human rights of minorities the General Assembly passed in December 1992. Future official murderers and rapists will be carefully calibrating the seriousness of the Bosnian War Crimes Commission and the International Criminal Court recently created by the UN.

The generation of refugees as an expression of deliberate policy constitutes a particularly ugly form of political behavior. Relief agencies do not like to discuss murderous activities by tyrants, and diplomats usually tiptoe around "host" government sensitivities. The consequence has been virtual immunity for those who torment and displace thousands of innocents while good people clean up after their crimes. The United States should push its proposal to extend the concept of war crimes, left vague by the Nuremberg trials, to cover peacetime humanitarian crimes such as ethnic cleansing and deliberate creation of refugees. The community must find ways to make the costs of forcible civilian displacement far more credible in advance before pieces of the old USSR devour each other, Sudan's rulers further decimate non-Muslim populations or, more remotely, Hungarian ultranationalists some day trigger a catastrophic drive for "greater Hungary."

Peaceful Change. In the best of all worlds, compliance begins with obedience to law. In our second- or third-best world, a more relevant process is that of peaceful change.

The law works in disputes where the parties are prepared to compromise or, if given a fair hearing, to accept an impartial third-party judgment. Except for a Hitler or a Saddam Hussein, where the only remedy may be counterforce, states generally comply with international law to the extent the rules are considered fair.

The UN Genocide Convention, along with the Fourth Geneva Convention and its successors on laws of war, should be expanded to cover "slow-motion genocide" of the Yugoslav variety.

The problem arises when the reason for not accepting third-party adjudication or arbitrament is either mistrust of the dominant legal system or unvarnished insistence on winning. The International Court of Justice (ICJ) has had some successes in dealing with primarily legal questions, but a string of failures when the issue was really political, from disregard by Albania in 1949 of the Court's ruling in the Corfu Channel case, to the Nicaragua harbor-mining judgment of 1986, on which the United States, unlike even Communist Albania and Qadhafi's Libya, rejected the Court's jurisdiction. (The current argument before the Court between Bosnia and "Yugoslavia" is obviously not about law and will not be resolved there.)

Disputes that are not "justiciable" require not so much application of existing law as justice and equity. Article 14 of the UN Charter was drafted with the Versailles treaty's disastrous rigidity in mind, and the UN played a major role in the process of decolonization—a de facto peaceful change process. But the General Assembly was never intended to acquire "legislative" powers (except when asked by the foreign ministers to decide the disposition of the Italian colonies after World War II) and article 14 has been invoked only rarely.

Today pressures for changes in the map are being fueled by exploding national and ethnic passions—the pathological flip side of the world's glorious diversity. Some are purely racist, such as the rabid nationalism of Russian or Serb extremists. But some pressures for change reflect genuine grievances with a legitimate case for relief. Diplomats usually find such issues as welcome as a visit to a leper colony. But a long and lugubrious history argues against their squeamishness and in favor of significantly greater activism toward justice in advance of disaster. The needful motto—indeed the updated definition of peace itself—could usefully be "The dynamic management of change without war."

The International Court of Justice should dust off its rarely used capacity to deal with disputes in the fashion lawyers call *ex aequo et bono*, meaning applying equity and common sense rather than the letter of the law. There are already a few examples of the type of small panels of Security Council members advocated by Louis Sohn to work out equitable resolution of clashing claims before they become full-blown Council debates. Such peaceful change devices should be applied to allegations of injustice by both sides in Kashmir, permanent stalemate in Cyprus, denial of Kurdish national rights in Turkey and Iraq, and arguments about ownership of rich resources in the Spratley Islands dispute between half a dozen Asian and Southeast Asian states, all of which have the potential to explode.

Inconsistency and hegemonic power

Intervention in civil wars and other forms of domestic mayhem is, with the best of motives, going to violate the fourth cardinal rule of diplomacy (never get between a dog and a lamppost), and at best appear inconsistent. The Security Council enforced its no-fly zones in northern Iraq but turned a blind eye until spring 1994 to violations in Serbia; forcibly protected famine relief in Somalia but not Bosnia; defended Kuwait but not Azerbaijan. Burundi was doubtless as deserving as Haiti, but as Boutros Boutros-Ghali said, "The United Nations cannot solve every problem," while Under Secretary General James Jonah acknowledged that Rwanda but not Burundi got peacekeepers and money because "maybe they were first in line."[14] As with the rest of human life, consistency cannot be the major litmus test. It is not cynical but realistic to acknowledge that political triage is the likely prospect, and that the world is fortunate if the large matters—Iraqi aggression, starving children, the ozone layer, nuclear spread—are tackled by the community even while some lesser issues remain unresolved.

Today pressures for changes in the map are being fueled by exploding national and ethnic passions— the pathological flip side of the world's glorious diversity.

Another troublesome reality is the disparity between states' power, money, and influence. Even a modestly reformed international "law and order" system will appear to be dominated by the strong both in making and enforcing rules. There are times—Korea in 1950 and the Gulf in 1990—when the community agrees to meet aggression by naming one country as "executive agent" for the Security Council (the formula used in Korea). If in such extreme circumstances—cross-border aggression or domestic genocide—the system fails to respond, action on behalf of the community could be carried out by what I have dubbed a "coalition of the willing." Both U.S. leadership and coalition surrogates run counter to the principle/ fiction of sovereign equality. But only a minority of states are in a position to give leadership based on advanced technology, capital, educated and trained armed forces, and a democratic process that protects the rights of individuals against governmental abuse. Others resent the unique influence of the United States. But the precondition for any enforcement system is the power and logistical reach the United States alone commands.

The real danger is not U.S. domination but its withdrawal from the game. The future could look a lot more dangerous if setbacks and scapegoating in Somalia, Haiti, and Bosnia reversed the recent U.S. turn toward cooperative security, or if premature intervention fatigue allowed new breaches of the "civil peace" to turn into serious security threats. Nothing is more important than to persuade would-be violators that failure to enforce the community's rules in Bosnia, plus erratic behavior in Somalia and Haiti, have not switched on a green light for arson in other tinderboxes.

Intervention in civil wars and other forms of domestic mayhem is, with the best of motives, going to violate the fourth cardinal rule of diplomacy (never get between a dog and a lamppost).

In the turbulent wake of controversy over the cases from hell, Washington crafted a policy toward UN "peace operations." In part political damage-limitation with the help of rhetorical straw men ("We will never compromise military readiness to support peacekeeping . . . [or transfer] troops into a standing world army . . . the President will never relinquish his constitutional command authority over U.S. troops," etc.), the bottom line is continuity in policy toward selective involvement after "asking tough questions," getting the Pentagon to help pay, and demanding fairer assessments and more efficient management.[15] The United States in fact retains a unique role in providing logistical support (already anticipated in the so-called Prepo Afloat program of ship-borne floating equipment for an armored brigade whose mission includes disaster relief and humanitarian operations). But U.S. domestic agonies over the cases from hell would seem to confirm the wisdom of traditional UN peacekeeping policy under which, except for enforcement, UN policing units on the ground were drawn from countries other than Russia and the United States. The concept of impartial peacekeeping and peacemaking by "neutrals" may still have high political value even if it is no longer clear what they are neutral about, and even though they are backed by great-power logistics, air and sea cover, and Japanese money.

Saving the world from hell

Definitive conclusions drawn from recent events are likely to be misleading. After all, no one predicted the fantastic changes of recent years. Our age is a hinge of history, and the post–Cold War order is a work in progress. Winston Churchill once observed that "The United Nations was set up not to get us to heaven, but only to save us from hell." There is nothing wrong with the basic norms and ground rules contained in the present UN Charter, which provides ample machinery for prevention, deterrence, and enforcement. The fault, pace Shakespeare, is not in our stars but in our leaders and those of us they represent.

Despite setbacks and loss of nerve, the innovative collective measures of the early 1990s could in time become habit-forming, particularly if politicians keep their nerve and eschew the "Principle of the Dangerous Precedent," which says that nothing should ever be done for the first time.[16] Once again, as in 1945, the future hinges on the political imagination and moral authority of those in power. Absent those qualities, there is no UN, no law, and no order.

Notes

1. Broadcast of February 19, 1994, as reprinted in Douglas Jehl, "Clinton Says Serbs Must Fully Comply on Arms Deadline," *New York Times*, February 20, 1994, p. A-1.

2. As the *Economist* put it, "because world trade moves in all directions it needs a worldwide . . . set of rules, and a global . . . enforcement service." "The Trade Winds Shift," November 20, 1993, p. 15.

3. A nationwide random sample polled in February 1994 by National Research, Washington, D.C., found an overwhelming majority in support of the concept of UN peacekeeping, with 81 percent supporting operations in the event of gross human rights violations and 83 percent in favor in case of large-scale atrocities. Steven Kull and Clay Ramsay, "U.S. Public Attitudes on UN Peacekeeping, Part I Funding" (Program on International Policy Attitudes, Center for International and Security Studies at Maryland, School of Public Affairs, University of Maryland, College Park, Md., March 7, 1994), p. 5.

4. Samuel P. Huntington, "The Clash of Civilizations?" *Foreign Affairs* 72 (Summer 1993), p. 39.

5. Elaborated in *Rethinking International Governance* by the present author and Harlan Cleveland (Minneapolis: Humphrey Institute, University of Minnesota, 1988).

6. The long half-life of such proposals is illustrated by some much earlier attempts in this realm. See, for example, the author's *International Military Forces: The Question of Peacekeeping in an Armed and Disarming World* (Boston: Little, Brown, 1964), and "Peacekeeping and Peacemaking," *Foreign Affairs* 44 (July 1966).

7. Boutros Boutros-Ghali, *An Agenda for Peace: Preventive Diplomacy, Peacemaking and Peace-Keeping* (New York, N.Y.: United Nations, 1992).

8. The arguments were explored in the author's "Nuclear Spread and World Order," *Foreign Affairs* 53 (July 1975).

9. Lewis A. Dunn, "Rethinking the Nuclear Equation: The United States and the New Nuclear Powers," *The Washington Quarterly* 17 (Winter 1994), pp. 5–25.

10. John Barry, "Soon, 'Phasers on Stun,'" *Newsweek*, February 7, 1994, pp. 24–26.

11. As the German foreign minister, Klaus Kinkel, put it: "There is preventive

diplomacy, but in practice we often see too little of it, too late." Quoted in Craig R. Whitney, "Europe Seeks Ways to Put Out Its Brushfires," *New York Times*, December 2, 1993.

12. According to David Binder in "U.S. Policymakers on Bosnia Admit Errors in Opposing Partition in 1992," *New York Times*, August 29, 1993.

13. Apart from closing a memory gap, this is probably a principal value of such systems as the CASCON computerized conflict analysis program developed by the author and Allen Moulton, already used experimentally by the UN, government agencies, and scholars. See the author's "Computerizing Conflicts," *Foreign Service Journal*, June 1988.

14. Reported in the Boston *Globe*, October 28, 1993. According to Paul Lewis, Washington blocked efforts to send a UN force to Burundi. "Reluctant Peacekeepers: Many U.N. Members Reconsider Role in Conflicts," *New York Times*, December 12, 1993.

15. As described by National Security Adviser Anthony Lake in "The Limits of Peacekeeping," *New York Times*, February 6, 1994.

16. F.M. Cornforth, quoted by Peter J. Gomes in "Back in the Military Closet," *New York Times*, May 22, 1993.

8

The United Nations
Is a Positive Force

Thomas B. Morgan

Thomas B. Morgan is president of the United Nations Association of the USA, a national, nonpartisan membership organization.

The United Nations has been blamed for failing to end the wars in Bosnia and Somalia during its interventions in those countries, though its only mission in each case was to provide humanitarian aid. Those who criticize the United Nations should remember that the U.N. is made up of individual member states, all of whom share the responsibility for failed missions. The U.N. should receive credit for its success in saving the lives of refugees, reducing poverty, and stopping violence.

Give the United Nations a break. For all the passionate and disparate voices decrying its failure in Bosnia, let's at least note that the role of the United Nations in that beleaguered part of the world was, from the beginning, one of humanitarian relief, not defense of the Bosnian government, and that the role of the world body in dealing with conflicts in the Balkans (or anywhere else) is determined not by some independent, supranational organization but by the 15 sovereign nations that compose the Security Council. Even among these, the decision-making primarily is in the hands of just five nations—the permanent members (China, France, Russia, the United Kingdom and the United States), each of which possesses the power to veto any decision.

The international community's decisions

Thus, all decisions concerning Bosnia—from the initial decision to provide humanitarian relief for civilians caught in a war zone to the subsequent decision to provide some protection for relief workers who were at mortal risk, to the yet later decision to limit the war's impact on civilians by creating areas designated as safe havens—all were made by the international community, in general, and the United States, the European Community and Russia, in particular. (For its part, China is an almost

Thomas B. Morgan, "U.N. as Strong as Its Members," *Insight*, August 28, 1995. Reprinted with permission from *Insight*. Copyright 1995 by The Washington Times Corporation.

silent partner, with little direct interest in Balkan affairs.) Though specu-
lation may be useless, it is fair to assume that had there been no United
Nations, those same nations well might have made the same collective
decisions and, today, be in the same mess of shame and regret. Indeed,
without the United Nations, the crisis still might be unfolding with far
greater brutality and bloodshed.

The United Nations exists because the 185 nations that have joined
the world organization desire to share the costs of addressing global problems. Whether they are facing naked aggression, environmental degrada-
tion, illicit drug trafficking or a health pandemic, solutions invariably en-
tail a financial cost, a political cost and—all too often—a human cost.
Nations, even great nations like the United States, increasingly have
sought to share such costs with other nations. And having proved time
and again that collective action works, the United Nations has endured.

---

*Nations increasingly have looked upon the
United Nations as an indispensable part of the
solution to the toughest problems.*

The very success of the United Nations—to have survived 50 years
and to have prevailed from Korea to Kuwait and in so many social and
humanitarian arenas—has contributed to the disappointment about the
crisis in Bosnia. Since the mid-1980s, in particular, nations increasingly
have looked upon the United Nations as an indispensable part of the solution to the toughest problems, with Bosnia having emerged as one of
the very toughest. The political advantage of problem-solving through
the United Nations has been obvious. When the international community can address a measurable task, such as it has done successfully—
given diplomacy, sanctions and patience—in the Iran-Iraq War (1988),
Namibia (1989), El Salvador (1991), Cambodia (1993) and, most recently,
Mozambique (1995), all concerned may accept the accolades that accom-
pany such triumphs. And when, as in Somalia and Bosnia, the international community miscalculates and finds itself daunted by history and
conflicting interests, the United Nations can take the fall.

The end of collective security?

But not so neat. The Bosnia crisis well could mean the beginning of the
end of our international system of collective understanding, balanced by
U.S. power and U.N. ideals, that has inspired the search for peace for the
last 50 years. Its success or failure depends more than ever upon the nations that support it. And its future depends on the wisdom of those who
would use it.

The American public quite clearly sees the Balkan wars as a problem
for the United Nations to handle, not the United States alone. That
means sharing decisions—and risks—with other countries. Trying to rec-
oncile divergent views within one government is not easy; trying to do it
among several governments is even more cumbersome. But no one can
say with confidence that America alone knows how to solve the Bosnia

fighting; even the United Nations' harshest critics in Washington dare not suggest that the United States assume responsibility for the consequences if it employs unilateral policies that fail.

When Americans are willing to acknowledge this, they will realize that the United Nations, which is called a failure in Bosnia, must include the United States. Americans then will find it easier to focus on what the nations of the world still might do together before it is too late. And then act.

9

The United States Should Support the United Nations

The Defense Monitor

The Defense Monitor *is the publication of the Washington, D.C.-based Center for Defense Information, an organization that evaluates the U.S. military.*

The United States has long favored working with other nations to keep peace and enhance international security because this approach imposes fewer monetary and human costs on the United States than do unilateral defense efforts. In the past, the United Nations has served the United States well as a forum for these joint actions. In recent years, however, the United Nations has become mired in bureaucracy and financial mismanagement. The United States must take the lead to encourage the reforms that will allow the United Nations to remain an effective force for international peace.

Fifty years ago on June 26, 1945, 51 war-weary nations led by the United States created the United Nations, entrusting to it the role of maintaining or, if necessary, imposing world peace. This hope for a lasting peace, given renewed urgency by man's newly acquired ability to destroy the planet with the awesome power of atomic weapons, rapidly faded as the ideological battle between democracy and totalitarianism froze relationships between the two superpowers and their allies around the globe.

Costs of the Cold War

The cost of this 45-year stalemate was high:

- In the 149 wars between the end of World War II and 1992, more than 123 million people died. Two-thirds of the victims were noncombatants.
- In 1992, over 18 million people were still refugees relying totally on UN or private relief agencies.
- From the end of the Korean War to the fall of the Berlin Wall in

"The United Nations at Fifty: A Force for the Future," *Defense Monitor*, January 1996. Reprinted courtesy of the Center for Defense Information, Washington, D.C.

1989, the U.S. spent $12 trillion for defense, a price we thought necessary—and thus were willing to pay—to prevent an even more expensive and ghastly nuclear war with the Soviet Union and its allies.

The spread of arms

The catalyst for these horrible events was the indiscriminate selling or giving of billions of dollars worth of conventional arms to Third World nations or subnational groups who were pawns in the battle between the U.S. and the former USSR. During this period, the UN's ability to fulfill its mandate frequently was hostage to the veto power of one or another permanent Security Council member—China, France, Great Britain, the USSR, and the U.S. Thus in its first 45 years the UN initiated only 18 peace missions.

Since 1990, however, free of the artificial constraints of the Cold War, the UN has been testing—while simultaneously being tested on—its ability to support an expanded number and variety of peace operations. In this short period, the UN initiated 20 new peace missions. Military personnel wearing the UN "blue beret" or "blue helmet" rose from 10,000 to over 73,000 in 1994 and now number about 66,000.

International peace and security

Ever mindful of the failure of the League of Nations to prevent or end wars after World War I, the original 51 signers of the UN Charter made international peace and security the foremost mission of the new world forum. Yet for fifty years the promise of "no more wars" has been broken more often than honored. Thus nations of all sizes formed alliances, built up their military establishments with new—and increasingly more deadly—weapons, and continued the slaughter on battlefields both old and new.

On the core issue, the driving preoccupation of the original 51 signers to avoid a World War III fought with atomic weapons, the UN frequently served as an important, neutral meeting place for discussions aimed at easing international tensions before they escalated.

While the Cold War hindered the UN's international security mandate, it did achieve progress in its humanitarian and disaster relief roles. In fact, the success of the UN in these endeavors created a very favorable impression of the UN among Americans and won it much support in the United States.

The respect garnered from these nonviolent actions is now being tested in the U.S. and elsewhere by the burdens of the multiple UN interventions in civil as well as international conflicts. After 50 years, with 38 peace missions requiring from 1 to 28,000 personnel, and with membership now at 185 nations, the question confronting the world is not the survival of the UN but how it can be—and must be—reformed and reenergized to become a truly "united" entity able to achieve international peace through collective security.

The concept of "collective security" is not easily achieved among 185 nations. Forces for UN peace operations come together with different weapons, training, and support, conditions that strain even the most professional leaders. Nonetheless, such coalitions have had success as peacekeepers.

Despite the obvious point that collective security can save both

American lives and American treasure, some believe that we should not rely on a UN that might not always act in the perceived interests of the U.S. Framed in this light, collective security becomes more a stepchild to be employed when convenient for U.S. policy rather than the first recourse to lead international efforts to prevent or restrain violence.

The cost of policing the future world

It is easy with hindsight to criticize the UN's first 50 years; it is significantly harder to project what will happen in its next half century. Right now we are witness to a plethora of seemingly unending religious or ethnic based convulsions in the developing "Third World." Similar violent struggles for economic opportunity and political liberty also are retarding progress in many of the newly autonomous states of the former USSR and, tragically, in the former Yugoslavia.

How much more expensive a unilateral U.S. "peacekeeping" policy would be is not hard to gauge. U.S. military spending is still at 1980 Cold War levels and is planned to increase.

Well into the 1996 Fiscal Year (FY96) the Administration and Congress were still wrangling over the Pentagon's $264 billion budget. Yet they begrudge paying just over one-half of 1% of that military budget—some $1.5 billion—in dues and assessments for UN operations that were backed by the U.S. in the Security Council and started under both Republican and Democratic presidents. Put another way, in 1995 the U.S. spent $647 on our own military for every $1 we contributed for UN or UN-sponsored international peacekeeping.

This gross imbalance reflects a general inability within the Administration and Congress to recognize that the U.S. can, at significantly less cost, wield great influence over world events and achieve U.S. policy goals by remaining fully engaged in planning and implementing UN peace operations. Not only is such engagement cheaper, it allows us the luxury of influencing events with minimal commitment of U.S. military personnel. Of 66,000 military men and women currently on duty with the UN around the world, only 3,300 are Americans. Even this number of American military personnel is a break with past practice when, because of intense rivalry between the superpowers, few if any U.S. or Soviet forces were part of UN operations.

But the real surprise for many analysts and public opinion surveyors is that the U.S. public in general continues to support American participation in UN collective security missions. Even the increased "UN bashing" by politicians of both parties has failed to deflect this consensus. However, when the public is asked about supporting specific missions such as Bosnia and possibly the Golan Heights, the responses are less positive and can swing against a mission if the President fails to convince the voters that participation is in the U.S. national interest.

Reforming for efficiency and effectiveness

As with our own government, probably the major needed reform is streamlining the UN bureaucracy. A key element of this reform would transform the UN's core structures—Security Council, General Assembly, and Secretariat—to better reflect the diversity of the world community they serve. For example, many support permanent status on the Security Council for Japan, the second largest contributor to the UN, and Germany, Europe's economic "engine." Some even support a general expansion of the Security Council to include major regional powers on a semipermanent basis if they support the UN financially and militarily.

Beyond a carefully revised Security Council, the increased use of the UN to avert, restrain, or intervene in disputes between and within nations calls for improved military planning capabilities under the direction of the Security Council. The long-dormant Military Staff Committee, composed of the senior military officers of the five permanent Security Council members, is the logical candidate to implement this reform. Needed expertise could be provided by using active and retired military staff on temporary "loan" from the five permanent Security Council nations.

A UN military force

A more contentious reform involves the creation of a standing UN military or mixed civilian-military quick reaction force whose main function would be to respond to growing international and even intrastate tensions and incipient warfare. Such a force, which would act only when directed by the Security Council, is usually described in equipment terms as "light to medium" units with wheeled armored personnel carriers, light artillery and counter-battery radars, transport and armed helicopters, and combat engineer equipment including necessary bridging equipment.

In addition to military personnel for a quick reaction force—all volunteers released for UN duty by their governments—civilian or nation building components of the force would include civil affairs and psychological warfare experts; medical and civil engineer teams; judicial, constitutional, and electoral advisers; and, where famine is imminent, humanitarian relief specialists followed by agronomists to help farmers expand indigenous food production.

The size and mix of skills within the quick reaction force would be determined by the Security Council (where the U.S. has veto power) in each case requiring UN assistance. Personnel for the entire force would be approximately 10,000–15,000 troops *plus* necessary headquarters and support troops.

The original 51 signers of the UN Charter made international peace and security the foremost mission of the new world forum.

Significantly, the reaction force should be headed by a civilian with the military commander as his deputy. If a developing situation required heavier military forces—as when an original peacekeeping mission becomes peace enforcement—the Security Council would call for regular national military units to intervene under UN auspices and "stabilize" the working environment for humanitarian and other aid.

Establishing a credible, permanent UN quick reaction force would offer nation-states the option to reduce their own military establishments and budgets. How much could safely be cut depends, of course, on each nation's perception of threats from its neighbors and its confidence in the Security Council's ability to respond effectively to calls for assistance against aggression from without or civil war within.

What is most disheartening is the inability of U.S. decision makers to envision objectively the "world policeman" role that a well trained, well supported, quick reaction UN force could play in place of the U.S.

Logically, with the UN assuming this role, the U.S. could reduce its active forces and military budget just as our closest allies have already done. Instead, and with significant congressional backing, the Pentagon is trying to expand its missions to serve as the primary instrument of U.S. foreign policy even though military factors have given way to economic ones as the long term key to overall national security.

Once the public concludes that supporting UN peace operations is less costly than maintaining the current full range of U.S. unilateral military forces, public pressure to reduce the cost and size of the U.S. military may well increase.

Sovereignty: national security or international security?

One key argument by opponents of U.S. participation in UN peace operations is the "loss of sovereignty." What they ignore is the fact that long before the collapse of the bipolar world, America and many other nations were accepting *de facto* limits on their sovereignty in such major areas as communications, finance, trade, and the environment, to name only a few. Just as the "pooling" of national sovereignty in these areas has unquestionably improved living conditions for millions of people worldwide, many now believe the next significant limitation should apply to nation-state military budgets and force structures.

If defense pooling became a viable alternative to national military forces equipped with the latest high technology armaments, more resources could be shifted to programs for social, medical, and human development. The U.S. could safely reduce its military forces and still remain the world's best armed, best led, and best trained military.

But even those Americans who recognize the increasing and mutual interdependency of nations are hesitant to endorse a global "pooling" of national military forces. The sticking point is the ability of the UN to form a credible military force strong enough to guarantee protection of the territorial integrity of all nation-states. This is a crucial, pragmatic consideration, because leaders of nation-states will not place their trust in an international military force that is judged incapable of timely response to threats of or actual invasion by another country.

The UN frequently served as an important, neutral meeting place for discussions aimed at easing international tensions before they escalated.

If, however, leaders believe the UN would be uniformly responsive in sending forces to deter military action by others, the savings generated from reducing active military forces worldwide would be enormous.

Within the context of U.S. involvement in UN peace operations, probably the greatest hurdle is the question of command of military forces operating under UN mandate. Since Somalia, some have falsely raised alarms that the U.S. is surrendering its sovereignty when U.S. forces come under the operational control of a non-U.S. or even a non-NATO officer.

When substantial numbers of U.S. troops are part of a larger force operating under UN mandate, the entire force is usually commanded by an American. However, when contributing smaller units to non-U.S. dominated or NATO multinational efforts (as we did for the UNPROFOR mission in the former Yugoslavia), common sense suggests that U.S. troops come under the operational control of the appointed UN commander until the assigned mission is completed. Such arrangements do not involve U.S. sovereignty because the President always retains command authority for U.S. forces.

The public's apparent ambivalence on this question is fueled by politicians who profess to see no difference between "command" and "operational control." If policy makers would forcefully and publicly differentiate between "command" (never surrendered) and "control" (for a specific mission or period of time), the benefits of multinational peace operations might receive increased public support. The continuing failure of our elected officials to make this case may someday come back to haunt American foreign policy.

> *The U.S. can, at significantly less cost, wield great influence over world events and achieve U.S. policy goals by remaining fully engaged in planning and implementing UN peace operations.*

Regardless of how one considers the role and the successes and failures of the UN, most informed observers agree that the Achilles heel of the organization is its finances. In this regard, the U.S. example is hardly commendable while we owe the UN $1.5 billion. But the U.S. is hardly alone: 80 nations have failed to pay all their assessments. In itself this operates as a significant inhibitor for new UN peace operations.

Proposals to rectify UN funding shortfalls include a "UN tax" on international activities such as air travel, arms sales, and currency transactions. None of these options are currently under serious consideration since each would remove the Security Council's critical budget oversight and its ability to veto any peace operation that one or more permanent members do not want to undertake.

All these reforms—a streamlined bureaucracy, a more predictable base for its revenues, and closer scrutiny by the Security Council of new peace missions before it commits resources—will take time and effort to achieve. Critics and supporters alike understand that the important point right now is to develop unstoppable momentum for these reforms. As goals are achieved, the resulting perception that the UN is effective will create growing confidence favorable to early UN or UN sponsored diplomatic and economic interventions that resolve issues before the disputants resort to the threat or the actual use of arms.

As we leave this, the most devastating century in human history, we ought to reflect on the price the world paid in the form of dead, wounded, starving, and displaced men and women whose talents have been irreplaceably lost.

We need not, we cannot, allow the new century to replicate the old. The UN must be equipped now with the resources and the authority to act to preserve peace. What it will be able to do 50 years from now depends in part on how we adjust to the continuing evolution of international relations in an interdependent world community. Under strong U.S. leadership, the UN will become what its founders hoped: the institution of first—rather than of last—resort in the quest for a world at peace.

10

The United States Must Continue to Participate in U.N. Peacekeeping

Madeleine K. Albright

Madeleine K. Albright is U.S. ambassador to the United Nations.

The United States must be able to act alone if its security is threatened. However, joint peacekeeping operations through the United Nations cost less, involve fewer American troops, and appear more politically legitimate than unilateral military action. The war with Iraq is an example of how effective joint operations can be, and the United States should continue to participate in such efforts. The United States must oppose those who argue that U.N. peacekeeping is too expensive or too dangerous.

The United States needs a UN that helps address international problems before they grow and endanger our security and economic well-being. American support for, and occasional participation in, United Nations peacekeeping operations contributes to that objective.

The UN serves American interests

While the ultimate guarantor of our security remains our capacity to act forcefully and, if we must, unilaterally, United Nations peace operations can also serve our interests. In fact, the more able the UN is to contain or end conflict, the less likely it is that we will have to deploy our own armed forces.

Administrations from both parties have long looked upon UN peace operations as a means for gaining international participation, financing and backing for objectives we support. Today, of the more than 67,000 UN peacekeepers deployed in 17 missions, less than two percent are American. American forces comprise less than five percent of all UN peacekeepers. Yet, each operation is serving a purpose or purposes of interest to the United States.

Madeleine K. Albright, "Alone in a Dangerous World," *National Debate*, March/April 1995. Reprinted by permission of the author and publisher.

For example, on the Golan Heights, more than 1,000 UN troops ensure the observance of a cease-fire between Israel and Syria, keeping open the possibility of a breakthrough in Middle East peace negotiations. Along the Iraq-Kuwait border, a 1,200-person observer mission (financed largely by Kuwait) monitors Iraqi troop movements, demonstrating the world's continued resolve against the expansionist ambitions of Saddam Hussein.

In Haiti, a U.S.-led operation has helped to restore democratic processes to an impoverished nation close to our shores, has stemmed a tide of refugees to the U.S., and has helped to alleviate human rights abuses and suffering. When this operation is turned over to the UN, the number of U.S. troops participating—and the U.S. share of costs—will be reduced by more than half.

And in Bosnia, the UN has worked in a sometimes strained partnership with NATO to restore a semblance of normal life to Sarajevo, prevent mass slaughter in "safe areas," and maintain a humanitarian lifeline that has kept hundreds of thousands alive, despite bitter fighting. These efforts, welcomed by the Bosnian government, have helped preserve the possibility of a negotiated end to the fighting.

UN operations cost comparably little

Most UN peace operations are small. More than half consist of fewer than 200 observers or peacekeepers. The missions that now require more than 2,000 personnel are those in the former Yugoslavia, Rwanda and Lebanon. The only other operations of this size are in Haiti and Angola.

The financial side of UN peacekeeping operations is equally modest. The total assessed cost to the United States of all UN peacekeeping operations in fiscal year 1994 was roughly $1 billion, about $4 per American, and less than one-half of one percent of our foreign policy and national security expenditures. U.S. law mandates that, as of October 1, 1995, our share of UN peacekeeping operations will drop from more than 30 percent of current costs to 25 percent. Further, direct U.S. participation in UN peace operations is limited. As of January 1, 1995, the U.S. ranked 27th among nations in the number of troops participating.

Overall, UN peacekeeping contributes to a world that is more stable, free, productive and secure than otherwise would be the case. We do not look to the UN to defend America's vital interests, nor can we expect the UN to be effective where the swift and decisive application of military force is required. But, in many circumstances, the UN will provide options for diplomatic, political and military action we would not otherwise have. It enables us to influence events without assuming the full burden of costs and risks. And it lends the weight of law and world opinion to causes and principles we support.

Withdrawing UN support would be a mistake

In the late 1940s and early 1950s, there were many who called for the U.S. to abandon the UN because it had failed to prevent the Korean War. There is a similar frustration now because the UN was unable to halt Rwandan genocide, transform Somalia or bring peace with justice to the Balkans.

We are finding that few international conflicts offer the clarity provided by Iraq's invasion of Kuwait—where the aggression was clear, the stakes included oil and the possibility of a madman equipped with nuclear arms, the military terrain was favorable, the enemy was isolated, the finest armed forces in the world—ours—were fully engaged, and the bills were being paid by someone else. Increasingly, threats to stability are not clear, but devilishly complex: violence caused not by international aggression, but by civil war; fragile cease-fires that do not hold; extremist political movements within strategic states; or ethnic violence that spills unpredictably across national lines.

The United States needs a UN that helps address international problems before they grow and endanger our security and economic well-being.

However, on Capitol Hill, prescriptions now circulating for responding to these challenges would remove the UN as an option. The rationale is bewildering. Sponsors say the cost of UN peace operations is too high, that the readiness of our armed forces is harmed by its support of UN operations. The irony is that if we put the UN out of business, our costs will go up, not down. We will have to act on our own more often. The wear and tear on our military will be *greater*, not less.

Those who advocate, in the words of one, "ending UN peacekeeping as we know it," should consider with care what would happen if they got their wish.

We could expect that:

• First, existing peace operations would be disrupted at great peril to world peace. I can think of few quicker ways to undermine global stability than to rip UN peacekeepers out of Cyprus, Lebanon, and the border between Kuwait and Iraq.

• Second, there would be no new or expanded UN peace operations. In some cases, this would represent dollars saved. But successful operations, such as those in Namibia, El Salvador, Cambodia and Mozambique, reduce long term costs. They permit refugees to return home and create conditions under which domestic economies may rebuild. As Representative Ben Gilman wrote to the President, the cost of an expanded peace operation in Angola would certainly not exceed the amount currently devoted to humanitarian relief.

• Third, monitoring the actions of major regional powers would be more difficult. Today, for example, small UN observer missions provide a useful window on events in Georgia and Tajikistan, where Russian peacekeeping forces are deployed. Verifying that peacekeeping is being conducted in accordance with international principles and with respect for the sovereignty of local governments would be complicated by the lack of a UN presence.

• Finally, if America pulls the plug on UN peacekeeping, our ability to lead at the UN will be seriously damaged. Our influence would surely diminish over decisions ranging from maintaining sanctions against rogue states to UN reform to ensuring greater balance within the General Assembly on resolutions affecting the Middle East. And our ability to argue that other nations should meet their obligations to the UN and to international law would be undermined.

With strong American leadership, the UN can be a valuable force for law and the extension of political freedoms. When all is said and done, I am confident that we will have bipartisan support for providing that leadership. The nature of the world today demands it. Key leaders on Capitol Hill—most of them anyhow—understand it. The American people expect it. And the best interests of our country require it.

11

The United Nations Is Not a Threat to American Sovereignty

Barbara Crossette

Barbara Crossette is a staff writer for the New York Times.

The United Nations, for most of its existence, has been perceived as a benign, freedom-promoting organization. Some Americans now worry that the United Nations is an alien entity that threatens U.S. sovereignty and security. The United Nations is not becoming a world government and cannot threaten the sovereignty of the United States because it lacks military might and political power.

Overnight, a message was left on an office answering machine at the United Nations. Is it true, a West Coast caller wanted to know, that the organization has changed its motto from "Swords into Plowshares" to "Peace and Security"?

Say what?

A return call elicited an explanation: In several Biblical passages, the caller said, "peace and security" is a code message signaling the apocalypse. Was the United Nations saying the end is nigh?

Not likely. The United Nations, which hasn't gotten around to choosing a motto in 50 years, is not very good at predictions either. A meeting announced for 10:30 A.M. might start any time after 11 or 3 P.M. or maybe not at all. Things that could get done on Monday morning are still unfinished on Friday night. And the end of the world could come and go long before any three people in authority agree on how to phrase a news release—which would then be held up in translation into six languages. That is, if the warning weren't classified secret.

'World government'

The United Nations' relations with the United States, never smooth, have turned bizarre. The April 19, 1995, bombing of the Federal building in

Oklahoma City has riveted the nation's attention on right-wing groups who behold the United Nations as a dark and sinister force. United Nations officials now return the favor by viewing much of America as pretty weird and dangerous too. The clash of perceptions might be truly funny if it weren't so deadly serious. It has already begun to translate into political action.

In Congress, the evident resentment in the heartland makes it easier for legislators to seek wholesale cuts in American support for the United Nations and its agencies. And pressure groups are able to force the cancellation of an event as homegrown as the Conference of the States—a gathering in Colorado Springs for leaders of state governments—on the strength of rumors that a conspiracy is afoot to impose a "world government." At the golden anniversary celebration of the signing of the United Nations Charter in San Francisco on June 26, 1995, not a single elected Republican, including Gov. Pete Wilson of California, was politically brave enough to attend.

A top United States diplomat was asked in Seattle if white-painted vehicles seen in Montana meant a United Nations takeover of the state.

At a time when this organization created almost entirely by the United States should be looking ahead to challenges as great as or greater than those that greeted its birth in 1945, it is instead fending off a barrage of incredible grassroots allegations. Out there in America are people who challenge anyone with international credentials. A top United States diplomat was asked in Seattle if white-painted vehicles seen in Montana meant a United Nations takeover of the state. A United Nations official on a speaking tour was confronted with the accusation that American military equipment had been reconfigured to conform more easily to the arsenal of the organization. In San Francisco, a man commented that those who fear the United Nations most may have some special sense— "like animals who can see in the dark," he said—to discern a terrible threat from this force on the East River whose most efficient employees are the short-order cooks in the cafeteria.

Dark rumors fill the vacuum of ignorance about an institution that has largely vanished from American textbooks. So a mirage of blue-and-white tanks can loom easily behind a Unesco sign declaring Yellowstone a "world heritage site." Sinister black helicopters bringing a new world order—order? at the U.N.?—are spotted over towns and farms. Some United Nations officials say they have taken to subscribing to hate literature just to keep abreast of thinking in the enemy camp.

"Who is this Boutros?" a San Francisco man asked recently as Secretary General Boutros Boutros-Ghali's motorcade went by. "We hear he's wanted in his own country, and that's why he stays here."

The United Nations cannot be absolved of blame for the predicament it faces. Organizationally, it seems incapable of projecting itself when its accomplishments are genuine, and then complains when journalists won't do the job for it. Obfuscation can be attributed in large part to the attitude of many member nations accustomed to harassing the press and thinking of information as a tool to be wielded and manipulated by the state, not a commodity to be shared. Mr. Boutros-Ghali, unlike at least two of his predecessors, has no American expert in his immediate entourage (which critics on his staff call an Oriental court) and thus, it seems, no effective intermediary to the United States.

Increased security

In the United States, a country where people like their politics personal, the United Nations is a faceless glass box peopled by mysterious foreigners speaking in tongues. United Nations officials and diplomats are perplexed and flabbergasted.

"We don't have—thank heaven!—these sort of extreme right-wing fringe groups, much, in Britain," said Sir David Hannay, Britain's representative. Though Europe has isolationism and neo-Fascism, he said, "it doesn't take on such an anti-U.N. manifestation as here, perhaps because the U.N. is here, and not there."

The United Nations—with no standing army, tanks or even mess kits, only flags to lend to forces contributed by member nations—is often as afraid of its American enemies as they are of it. Offices of the United Nations are getting many more phone threats. Security has been stepped up at headquarters in New York and for appearances by the Secretary General both in the United States, where he now gets a Secret Service detail, and abroad, where he has been targeted by foreign terrorists. His itineraries are no longer revealed in detail.

> *The United Nations—with no standing army, tanks or even mess kits, only flags to lend to forces contributed by member nations—is often as afraid of its American enemies as they are of it.*

Mr. Boutros-Ghali, an Egyptian Coptic Christian married to an Egyptian Jew and an architect of the Camp David accords with Israel, is on virtually every militant Islamic group's death list. Even if not all the hostility is American, the venue of a free society carries obvious perils. United Nations officials are convinced that the World Trade Center bomb could well have been delivered to them. One of the men arrested in the attack had taken a tour of the United Nations three times in a day.

Ambassadors and officials go to seminars to talk about the phenomenon of the United Nations' war of words and perceptions with America and what to do if Congress really pulls enough financial support to cripple the organization. Ernst Sucharipa, Austria's representative, said Europeans are beginning to grumble about being the only fools who pay their share, and on time. "Why should we be the good guys?" he said. Add to that some exportable paranoia about World Government and Europe might also become a problem.

Michael Stopford, the British director of the United Nations information center in Washington, is on the radio talk-show circuit grappling regularly with American fears and trying, as he says, "to understand the special American perspective on life a long way from Washington and New York." Surprisingly, Americans respond reasonably once they hear him out, he said.

"The real red-flag phrase is world government," he said. "Immediately we have to say the U.N. has absolutely nothing to do with world government. The U.N.'s just there, to help you with all the horrid problems of today. You have to reassure them that the U.N. is not an international ogre."

12

Americans Support the United Nations

In These Times

In These Times is a left-wing journal of news and opinion.

A few Americans think that the United Nations threatens to take over the United States. Many others believe that the United States contributes too many troops and too much money to the U.N. Most of these critics, however, are misinformed and vastly overestimate the number of troops and the amount of money the United States gives to the U.N. When they are well informed, Americans support the U.N.'s goals of keeping the peace and promoting democracy.

After the United Nations was founded at the end of World War II, the idea of participating in an international organization as nominal equals with the Communist devil enraged right-wingers. For two decades the John Birch Society, the Cold War granddaddy of today's paranoid right, blighted the Western and Southern states, where it recruited most heavily, with billboards demanding that the United States get out of the U.N. And now, 50 years after its founding, the U.N. still haunts right-wing groups. Like John Birchers obsessed with an imagined invasion by Russian—or Chinese—troops, militia members today accuse Washington of planning to have the U.N. take over the United States and destroy our constitutional government.

America's perception of the U.N.

But paranoid right-wingers are not the only ones who seem to distrust the U.N. Indeed, those whose understanding of our society is formed by the commercial media might well assume that a majority of Americans share such views. Reading the papers and watching TV, one might suppose that most Americans not only feel that we are giving too much of our money to the U.N. but also that we should go it alone without being hamstrung by an organization of foreigners that places limitations on our status and

"Americans Support the Militia's Devil," *In These Times*, July 10, 1995. Reprinted by permission of *In These Times*.

freedom of action in international affairs.

This, indeed, is what some militia members feel. As Mike McKinzey, a self-proclaimed lieutenant in Missouri's 51st Militia, told Rebecca Shelton of the *Kansas City New Times*, the U.N. is taking over the country "inch by inch." For example, McKinzey was bothered recently when a U.S. helicopter pilot serving as part of the U.N. force in Korea was shot down by North Korean troops. What troubled McKinzey was the return of the pilot's body with a U.N. flag draped over his coffin. He also complained about the U.N. flag flying over the Truman Library; other members of the 51st Militia were disturbed when they saw the U.N. flag with American troops in Haiti.

These men believe that "nothing's going right" in the country. Crime is rampant, they say, yet guns are being taken away from law-abiding citizens. They believe that welfare is bankrupting the country. And they work hard to pay taxes only to see $20 billion sent to bail out Mexico. All these incidents remind McKinzey of his growing marginality and insecurity. "I'm tired of caring," he says. "I want to make my house payment and I'm not ashamed to say it . . . I could care less about Mexico."

American support for the U.N.

And yet, surprising as it may seem, the U.N. has strong support from the American people, especially when they are told the truth about our participation. This was verified in a poll by the Center for International and Security Studies at the University of Maryland. Some two-thirds of those polled support U.N. peacekeeping in principle, believe we should pay U.N. peacekeeping dues in full and support most peacekeeping operations. They not only approve contributing troops to U.N. peacekeeping, but significantly more than two-thirds approve of having them serve under a foreign U.N. commander if other nations have contributed more troops than has the United States.

And while 60 percent say that the United States is giving more than its share of troops to the U.N., that belief is based on ignorance of just how many we actually contribute. The median estimate of U.S. troop contribution among those polled was 40 percent. The median suggestion of an appropriate level was 30 percent. The actual level of U.S. contribution is only 4 percent.

The U.N. has strong support from the American people, especially when they are told the truth about our participation.

Similarly, 58 percent of those polled said that the United States is paying too much in dues to the U.N. But respondents offered a median estimate that 22 percent of the U.S. military budget goes to U.N. peacekeeping, and their median estimate of what was appropriate was 15 percent. The actual contribution is 1 percent. When told this, disapproval of the U.S. contribution among respondents dropped to 18 percent.

Interestingly, a majority of Americans supported the U.S. role in the restoration of President Aristide to power in Haiti and in the U.N. delivery of humanitarian aid to Somalia, though not the subsequent participation in the civil war there. And an overwhelming majority also said the U.N. should have intervened in Rwanda to stop the large-scale killings there.

Overall, it seems clear that when Americans are relatively well-informed they support democratic principles and humanitarian action. But it is also clear that, despite this being called the communications age, the commercial media keep Americans in a state of ignorance about the routine operations of our government. That's not really news, but it does help explain why movements like the militias have such an easy time recruiting frustrated and increasingly insecure citizens.

Organizations to Contact

The editors have compiled the following list of organizations concerned with the issues debated in this book. The descriptions are derived from materials provided by the organizations. All have publications or information available for interested readers. The list was compiled on the date of publication of the present volume; names, addresses, phone and fax numbers, and e-mail/internet addresses may change. Be aware that many organizations take several weeks or longer to respond to inquiries, so allow as much time as possible.

The Academic Council on the United Nations System (ACUNS)
The Watson Institute
Brown University
Box 1983
Providence, RI 02912-1983
(401) 863-1274
fax: (401) 863-3808
e-mail: ACUNS@brown.edu
internet: http://www.brown.edu/Departments/ACUNS

The ACUNS is an international association that is involved in the work and study of international organizations. The council maintains close working relationships with the U.N. Secretariat and hopes to strengthen the study of international organizations as they increase in number, activity, complexity, and importance. The ACUNS publishes a monthly newsletter as well as numerous reports and papers.

Campaign for U.N. Reform
420 Seventh St. SE, Suite C
Washington, DC 20003
(202) 546-3956
fax: (202) 546-3749
e-mail: dkraus@igc.apc.org

The campaign strives to compel the United Nations to reform its organizations. It engages in lobbying, works for the election of congressional candidates committed to U.N. reform, and rates representatives and senators on their votes on selected global issues. The campaign proposes a fourteen-point program to overcome existing weaknesses in the U.N. system. It publishes the brochures *The Fourteen-Point U.N. Reform Program*, *Global Burden Sharing*, and *Global Statesman Rating*.

Cato Institute
1000 Massachusetts Ave. NW
Washington, DC 20001
(202) 842-0200
fax: (202) 842-3490
internet: http://www.cato.org

The Cato Institute is a libertarian public policy research foundation dedicated to promoting limited government and individual liberty. It believes that the United Nations' lack of accountability to its member nations has led to corruption and mismanagement. The institute's numerous publications include the policy analysis "A Miasma of Corruption: The United Nations at Fifty."

Center for War/Peace Studies
218 E. 18th St.
New York, NY 10003
(212) 475-1077
fax: (212) 260-6384

The center conducts independent studies and proposes solutions for global problems. It is currently working on its Binding Triad proposal for global decision making, which would introduce a new voting system into the United Nations General Assembly. The center publishes the quarterly newsletter *Global Report* and the brochure *The Binding Triad.*

Committee on Teaching About the United Nations (CTAUN)
c/o **World Federalist Movement**
777 United Nations Plaza, 12th Fl.
New York, NY 10017
(609) 683-4561
fax: (609) 921-2586
e-mail: bwalker@igc.apc.org

The committee is composed of persons who have experience, knowledge, and interest in teaching about the United Nations. It compiles educational materials developed within the U.N. system and encourages teachers to teach their classes about the U.N. The committee publishes *Peace Works*, a teacher's guide to setting up a mini–United Nations project in schools.

The Heritage Foundation
214 Massachusetts Ave. NE
Washington, DC 20002-4999
(202) 546-4400
fax: (202) 546-0904

The foundation is a conservative public policy research institute dedicated to the principles of competitive free enterprise, limited government, individual liberty, and a strong national defense. Its numerous publications include the quarterly *Policy Review*, the Heritage Lecture Series, and the executive memoranda "The U.N. at Fifty: No Key to Peace," "Needed at the U.N.: More Secretary, Less General," and "The U.N. Tax: Not Now, Not Ever."

United Nations Development Programme (UNDP)
1 United Nations Plaza
New York, NY 10017
(212) 906-5315
fax: (212) 906-5001
e-mail: HQ@undp.org
internet: http://www.undp.org

The UNDP is committed to the principle that development is insepara-
ble from the quest for peace and human security and that the United
Nations must be a strong force for development as well as for peace. The
programme's mission is to help member nations achieve sustainable human development. It publishes "Beyond Aid: Questions and Answers for
a Post–Cold War World" and the quarterly magazine *Choices*.

World Constitution and Parliament Association (WCPA)
1480 Hoyt St., Suite 31
Lakewood, CO 80215
(303) 233-3548
fax: (303) 526-2185

The WCPA is an association of individuals and organizations in fifty
countries who are interested in establishing a federal world government
that would achieve world peace, solve problems, and work for the good
of humanity. It publishes the bimonthly newsletter *Across Frontiers* and
the paper "A Bill of Particulars: Why the U.N. Must Be Replaced."

World Federalist Association (WFA)
418 Seventh St. SE
Washington, DC 20003
(202) 546-3950
fax: (202) 546-3749

The WFA is an educational organization working to transform the
United Nations into a democratic world federation dedicated to ensuring peace, economic progress, and environmental protection. The association embraces the principle of voluntary, shared participation in an
ordered, manageable world. The WFA publishes the quarterly magazine
World Federalist.

World Federalist Movement (WFM)
777 United Nations Plaza, 12th Fl.
New York, NY 10017
(212) 599-1320
fax: (212) 599-1332
e-mail: wfm@igc.apc.org

The WFM is an international citizens organization founded in 1947 in Montreux, Switzerland. It is dedicated to promoting a strengthened, reformed United Nations to ensure a just world order. The WFM is currently active on such issues as U.N. Security Council reform, the promotion of an international criminal court, U.N. financing, and the democratization of the U.N. It publishes the *World Federalist News* twice a year and the *International Criminal Court Monitor* three times a year.

World Policy Institute
New School for Social Research
65 Fifth Ave., Suite 413
New York, NY 10003
(212) 229-5808
fax: (212) 229-5579

The institute is engaged in public policy research and public education on critical world problems and U.S. international policy. It develops initiatives that it believes reflect the shared needs and interests of all nations. The institute publishes the quarterly *World Policy Journal*, which often includes articles addressing the role of the United Nations.

Bibliography

Books

Peter R. Baehr and   *The United Nations in the 1990s*. New York: St. Martin's,
Leon Gordenker   1992.

Tom Barry   *The Next Fifty Years: The United Nations and the United
and Erik Leaver   States*. Albuquerque, NM: Resource Center Press, 1996.

Phyllis Bennis   *Calling the Shots: How Washington Dominates Today's UN*.
                          New York: Olive Branch Press; Brooklyn, NY: Interlink
                          Publishing, 1996.

Boutros Boutros-Ghali   *An Agenda for Peace*. New York: United Nations, 1995.

Roger Coate, ed.   *United States Policy and the Future of the United Nations*.
                          Washington, DC: Brookings, 1993.

William J. Durch   *The Evolution of UN Peacekeeping: Case Studies and
et al., eds.   Comparative Analysis*. New York: St. Martin's Press, 1993.

A.B. Fetherston   *Towards a Theory of United Nations Peacekeeping*. London:
                          Macmillan, 1994.

Cameron R. Hume   *The United Nations, Iran and Iraq: How Peacemaking
                          Changed*. Bloomington: Indiana University Press, 1994.

Amy Janello and   *A Global Affair: An Inside Look at the United Nations*. New
Brennon Jones, eds.   York: Jones & Janello, 1995.

Ian Johnstone   *Aftermath of the Gulf War: An Assessment of UN Action*.
                          Boulder, CO: Lynne Rienner, 1995.

John M. Lee, Robert   *To Unite Our Strength: Enhancing the United Nations Peace
von Pagenhardt, and   and Security System*. Lanham, MD: University Press of
Timothy W. Stanley   America; Washington, DC: International Economic
                          Studies Institute, 1992.

Stanley Meisler   *United Nations: The First Fifty Years*. New York: Atlantic
                          Monthly Press, 1995.

Linda Melvern   *The Ultimate Crime: Who Betrayed the UN and Why*.
                          London: Allison and Busby, 1995.

Michael Pugh, ed.   *Maritime Security and Peacekeeping: A Framework for United
                          Nations Operations*. Manchester, England: Manchester
                          University Press, 1994.

Steven R. Ratner   *The New UN Peacekeeping*. London: Macmillan, 1995.

J. Martin Rochester   *Waiting for the Millennium: The United Nations and the
                          Future of World Order*. Columbia: University of South
                          Carolina Press, 1993.

K.P. Saksena	*Reforming the United Nations: The Challenge of Relevance.* New Delhi: Sage, 1993.
United Nations	*The Guardian Soldier: On the Nature and Use of Future Armed Forces.* New York, 1996.
United Nations	*The United Nations and Cambodia 1991–1995.* New York, 1995.
United Nations	*The United Nations and El Salvador 1990–1995.* New York, 1995.

Periodicals

Addresses are provided for periodicals not indexed in the *Social Science Index*, the *Alternative Press Index*, the *Readers' Guide to Periodical Literature*, or the *Index to Legal Periodicals & Books*.

Gilbert Achcar	"United Nations—United States?" *International Viewpoint,* June 15, 1995.
Fouad Ajami	"What Really Happens to Lines in the Sand," *U.S. News & World Report,* June 3, 1996.
Madeleine K. Albright	"The United Nations, NATO, and Crisis Management," *U.S. Department of State Dispatch,* April 29, 1996.
James A. Baker	"Policy Challenges of UN Peace Operations," *Parameters,* Spring 1994. Available from the U.S. Army War College, Carlisle Barracks, Carlisle, PA 17013-5050.
J. Kenneth Blackwell	"World Wide Promotion of Human Rights," *Vital Speeches of the Day,* May 15, 1996.
John R. Bolton	"Toward a Unitary U.N.: Creating Political Order Out of Agency Chaos," *Common Sense,* Summer 1996. Available from 229 ½ Pennsylvania Ave. SE, Washington, DC 20003.
Boutros Boutros-Ghali	"Democracy: A Newly Recognized Imperative," *Global Governance,* Winter 1995. Available from 1800 30th St., Boulder, CO 80301.
Walter Clarke and Jeffrey I. Herbst	"Somalia and the Future of Humanitarian Interventions," *Foreign Affairs,* March/April 1996.
Contemporary Security Policy	"Security Policy Aspects of the United Nations," April 1994. Entire section on the U.N. Available from Newbury House, 890–900 Eastern Ave., Newbury Park, Ilford, Essex, IG2 7HH, UK.
Chester A. Crocker	"The Rules of Engagement in a New World: The U.S. Has Much at Stake in Its Strategy on U.N. Peacekeeping Operations," *Washington Post National Weekly Edition,* May 16–22, 1994.

98   At Issue

Javier Perez de Cuellar	"Reflecting on the Past and Contemplating the Future," *Global Governance*, May–August 1995.
Bob Dole	"Reign In United Nations Peacekeeping," *National Debate*, March/April 1995. Available from PO Box 5229, Arlington, VA 22205.
Michael W. Doyle	"Forcing Peace: What Role for the United Nations?" *Dissent*, Spring 1994.
Don Feder	"Michael New Versus the New World Order," *Conservative Chronicle*, February 7, 1996. Available from 9 Second St. NW, Hampton, IA 50441.
L. Fisher	"Breaking a Deadlock," *Macleans*, March 11, 1996.
Larry M. Forster	"Clear Mandate: Reforming US and UN Peace Operations," *Harvard International Review*, Summer 1996. Available from PO Box 401, Cambridge, MA 02238.
David P. Forsythe	"The UN and Human Rights at Fifty: An Incremental but Incomplete Revolution," *Global Governance*, September–December 1995.
John M. Goshko	"Downsizing the U.N. Is a U.S. Goal," *Washington Post National Weekly Edition*, July 1–7, 1996.
William Norman Grigg	"Follow the Leader? U.S. Soldiers Are Being Placed in Harm's Way—for the New World Order," *New American*, December 25, 1995. Available from 770 Westhill Blvd., Appleton, WI 54914.
Stefan Halper	"The United Nations' Second Half-Century: Time for an Overhaul," *USA Today*, September 1996.
Index on Censorship	"UN: Make or Break," September/October 1995.
International Journal on World Peace	"Making the United Nations Effective: Five Views on Its Fiftieth Anniversary," September 1994. Entire section on the U.N. Available from 2700 University Ave. West, Suite 47, St. Paul, MN 55114-1016.
Bryan T. Johnson	"Foreign Aid Wins Few Friends at the United Nations," *Heritage Foundation: F.Y.I.*, May 13, 1995. Available from 214 Massachusetts Ave. NE, Washington, DC 20002-4999.
Jeane Kirkpatrick	"Reliance on United Nations Is Dangerous," *Conservative Chronicle*, April 27, 1994.
Anthony Lake	"The Limits of Peacekeeping," *New York Times*, February 6, 1994.
Charles Lane	"Dues and Don'ts," *New Republic*, May 13, 1996.
Robert McClean	"Some Things the United Nations Does Not Do," *Christian Social Action*, June 1995. Available from 100 Maryland Ave. NE, Washington, DC 20002.

John F. McManus	"Who's in Charge of Our Military?" *New American*, May 30, 1994.
N. Morris	"Bombs of Wrath," *Macleans*, April 29, 1996.
N. Morris	"Buying Time," *Macleans*, April 1, 1996.
Joshua Muravchik	"What Use Is the UN?" *Commentary*, April 1996.
New American	"Coming Your Way: The United Nations, Global Government . . . and You!" April 3, 1995. Entire issue on the U.N.
New Internationalist	"Winds of Change: The United Nations at Fifty," December 1994. Entire issue on the U.N. Available from PO Box 1143, Lewiston, NY 14092.
Parameters	"UN Peace Support Operations," Spring 1994. Entire section on the U.N.
James Paul	"Deadbeat Nation," *Nation*, April 15, 1996.
George Perkovich	"Nehru's Ban, India's Bomb," *Nation*, June 10, 1996.
Julia Preston	"A Bloated World Body: Despite Efforts to Streamline, the United Nations Still Resists Shaping Up," *Washington Post National Weekly Edition*, January 30–February 5, 1995.
Rosemary Righter	"Making the United Nations Effective," *International Journal on World Peace*, September 1994.
Bruce Russett	"Ten Balances for Weighing UN Reform Proposals," *Political Science Quarterly*, vol. 111, no. 2, 1996.
Modesto Seara-Vasquez	"The UN Security Council at Fifty: Midlife Crisis or Terminal Illness?" *Global Governance*, September–December 1995.
U.S. Department of State Dispatch	"Fact Sheet: NATO Involvement in the Balkan Crisis," December 1995.
U.S. Department of State Dispatch	"Focus on the United Nations: UN Changes for the Better," February 19, 1996.
John L. Washburn	"United Nations Relations with the United States: The UN Must Look Out for Itself," *Global Governance*, January–April 1996.
Washington Quarterly	"Rethinking Peacekeeping," Summer 1995. Special section on the U.N. Available from MIT Press Journals, 55 Hayward St., Cambridge, MA 02142.
Washington Quarterly	"The United Nations and Civil Wars," Autumn 1994. Special section on the U.N.
Caspar W. Weinberger	"Elementary Lessons of Foreign Policy," *Forbes*, June 3, 1996.

Michael Wesley   "The Cambodian Waltz: The Khmer Rouge and United Nations Intervention," *Terrorism and Political Violence,* Winter 1995. Available from Newbury House, 900 Eastern Ave., London IG2 7HH, UK.

World Press Review   "Here's to You, Mrs. Robinson," July 1996.

Mortimer B. Zuckerman   "Adieu, Mr. Boutros-Ghali," *U.S. News & World Report,* May 27, 1996.

Index